Table of Contents

Table of Contents

About Dynamic Path

Dynamic Path has a simple mission statement: To help you pass your test and get ahead by providing high-quality study questions. Whether you're preparing for a real estate agent licensure or an AP exam, we want to help you succeed.

We believe in our content, and we offer 50 free practice questions for each of our exams on our site. You can take a sample test or study session with us online, and get the results emailed to you.

All exam modules are written and edited by experts in their field, and each practice question is accompanied by a detailed explanation.

There are several ways to learn with Dynamic Path. You can browse exams and learn on the site or through our mobile apps, available for iOS, Mac, Android, Kindle, and Windows.

Dynamic Path is a product of Upward Mobility, a 100% woman- and minority-owned company (SOWMBA-certified) based in Boston, MA. It was formed to create free and low-cost high-quality education and test preparation material that is witty, engaging, and adds value to the learning process. You can learn more about our social mission and values here, or read a message from one of our co-founders here. You can also learn more about our staff here.

If you have any questions, suggestions, or technical problems, feel free to email us at support@dynamicpath.com.

Happy studying!

Questions

Human Growth and Development

1.

Using motivation from 'within' is known as ____C____ .

    A. Inside motivation
    B. Interior motivation
    C. Intrinsic motivation
    D. Idealistic motivation

2.

Which of the following is _not_ an example of extrinsic motivation?

    A. Employee performance improves when wages are increased
    B. A sleep apnea patient follows a strict sleep hygiene plan
    C. Children finish a task more quickly if they are promised candy
    D. A student studies more on a test to make the highest grade in the class

Counseling Process

1.

Which of the following socioeconomic factor could affect the outcome of therapeutic counseling? Choose all that apply.

(A.) Lack of transportation
B. Lack of intrinsic motivation
(C.) Lack of positive <u>cultural</u> norms for entering therapy
D. None of the above   *Race / Ethnicity → Customs, traditions, values*

→ **2. There are five types of psychotherapeutic alliances. Pick two from the list below.**

study!

A. I-You relationships, Nonworking alliance
B. Transpersonal relationships, I-You relationships
C. Working alliances, You relationships
(D.) Reparative relationships, Inter-transpersonal relationships

Helping Relationships

1.

What is the meaning of transference/countertransference relationships? Choose all that apply.

A. A client transferring their relationship with another onto the therapist
B. The therapist transferring their relationship with another onto the client
C. Transferring the blame or outcome of behavior onto someone else
D. None of the above

Professional and Ethical Issues

1.

What is one instance that might cause a clinician to break the strong code of client confidentiality?

    A. Feeling the need to talk
    (B.) Duty to warn → *required by certain states*
    C. When the therapist is going on vacation
    D. All of the above

Human Growth and Development

1.

What three components make up all attitudes?

    A. Cognitive, Affective, Behavioral
    B. Emotional, Habitual, Disposition
    C. Health, Physical, Mental
    D. Nurture, Environment, Luck

2.

If when judging behavior of others we tend to emphasize internal personality factors over external situational causes; but when analyzing our own behavior, we emphasize internal personal attributions for our successes and ten to give external environmental attributions for our failures. This is known as _____ .

    A. Compensating
    B. Truth
    C. Self-serving bias
    D. Being different

3.

When we offer an explanation for behavior such as, "she was weak willed" or "he was intimidating," the term _____ is applied.

    A. Statement
    B. Attribution
    C. Generalization
    D. Accusation

4.

The age integration theory:

    A. Is meant to keep older people grouped together
    B. Refers to periods in one's life course
    C. Gives people of all ages the opportunity to pursue education, work, and leisure activities
    D. None of the above

5.

Increasing depression after age 65 may be caused by which of the following? Choose all that apply.

    A. The process of aging
    B. Change in social status
    C. Decrease in income
    D. None of the above

6.

What does socioeconomic status (SES) have to do with aging and health? Choose all that apply.

    A. A person can afford better medical care and food with a higher income
    B. More money makes everything look better, even aging
    C. If you have a better income, you can afford to travel or join a gym
    D. None of the above

Counseling Process

1. Treatment via multimodal therapy begins with a comprehensive assessment of seven areas. The questions and scales are used to identify both _____ and _____.

    A. Concerns and mental health
    B. Strength and problem areas
    C. Philosophies and beliefs
    D. None of the above

2. In multimodal therapy, people seem to respond best to interventions that target their _____?

    A. Preferred modalities
    B. Personality style
    C. Strengths
    D. Areas of concern

3. _____ and _____ are two useful techniques associated with multimodal therapy.

    A. Asking questions and listening
    B. Imagery and insight
    C. Bridging and tracking
    D. None of the above

4. In the BASIC ID acronym in multimodal therapy, what does the first "I" represent?

    A. Ideas
    B. Identify
    C. Imagery
    D. I don't know

5. Gestalt therapy may seem to be a sound approach for many people who seek treatment because they no longer have a sense of joy. Gestalt therapy is also well-suited for _____?

    A. People with several mental health disorders
    B. People with eating disorders
    C. People with schizophrenia
    D. People with mental retardation

6. Language plays an important part in Gestalt therapy, particularly the use of ____ and _____ questions.

    A. Reactive and thoughtful
    B. Useful and nonsense
    C. What and How
    D. Questions are not used in Gestalt Therapy

7. **In person-centered counseling, both _____ and _____ are vital.**

    A. Intervention strategies and therapeutic alliance
    B. Goals and therapeutic alliance
    C. Behavior and thought patterns
    D. All of the above

8. **In person-centered therapy, what does the clinician do?**

    A. Help clients with distorted thinking
    B. Create an environment that allows people to trust themselves
    C. Create behavioral interventions for the client to work on at home
    D. Interpret dreams, fantasies, and imagery.

Helping Relationships

1.

When is clinician self-disclosure appropriate? Choose all that apply.

A. Clinician self-disclosure is never appropriate
B. When it enhances the collaborative nature of the client-clinician relationship
C. When it provides a different perspective
D. None of the above

Counseling Process

1. The fundamental goal of existential therapy is helping people find _____, _____, and _____ in their lives.

    A. Value, meaning, and purpose
    B. Value, fulfillment, and meaning
    C. Hope, happiness, and structure
    D. Contentment, fulfillment, and happiness

2. In cognitive therapy, _____and _____ cognitions are steps toward a less distorted way of thinking.

    A. Recognizing and mapping
    B. Understanding and focusing on
    C. Disputing and replacing
    D. None of the above

Human Growth and Development

1.

"My physician didn't call to tell me the test results. She probably has bad news and doesn't want to tell me." is an example of what type of distorted thinking?

A. All or nothing thinking
B. Overgeneralization
C. Mental filter
D. Jumping to conclusions

Counseling Process

1. In cognitive therapy, sessions are carefully planned and structured to maximize their _____ and _____.

    A. Impact and efficiency
    B. Goals and direction
    C. Fairness and accuracy
    D. A and C

2. Judith Beck, a leading cognitive therapist, has recommended 10 procedures for an initial session. Which one of the answers below is not one of these procedures?

    A. Establish a meaningful agenda
    B. Identify and review presenting problems
    C. Lead the client in a series of free associations
    D. Establish goals

3. Before cognitive therapists move forward with interventions, they take the time to develop a _____.

    A. Hypothesis
    B. Case formulation
    C. Outline of interventions
    D. Time line of treatment

4. In behavior therapy, the first step in changing a behavior is describing that behavior in terms that are _____ and _____.

    A. Understandable and obtainable
    B. Specific and measurable
    C. Open and reliable
    D. Both B and C

5. In behavioral therapy, once the problem behaviors have been clearly described, a baseline can be obtained, reflecting the severity and frequency of the behaviors before treatment. What do both the client and clinician need to decide?

    A. How to measure the behavior
    B. Ways to record the measurement
    C. How the client feels about the behavior
    D. Both A and B

Assessment and Diagnosis

1. **With respect to crisis counseling, what is a crisis?**

   A. Single or recurrent problems that are overwhelming or traumatic
   B. A psychosocial development stage
   C. An episode of weakness
   D. All of the above

2. **Crisis counseling usually lasts _____.**

   A. Until all of the client's symptoms are resolved
   B. Until stabilization occurs and the client can resume normal functioning
   C. Usually one to three months
   D. Both B and C

3. **As a counselor, what other agencies could you work with in a crisis situation?**

   A. Law enforcement agencies
   B. FEMA
   C. State Health and Human Services
   D. All of the above

4. **After a disaster, special care must be taken in which population(s)?**

   A. Men and women
   B. Children and the elderly
   C. Teachers and construction workers
   D. No special care is given to any particular group

5. **What are some reasons to provide community outreach?**

   A. To reach an underserved population
   B. To increase public awareness
   C. To link resources with other agencies with common purpose
   D. All of the above

6. **Surveys have shown the elderly to be an underserved population in the area of mental health services. What can a mental health clinic provide to this population in the way of community outreach?**

   A. Psycho educational classes at the senior center
   B. Mental health information sent via traditional mail services
   C. Staff senior centers with counselors for brief solution-focused therapy
   D. All of the above

7. **Several funding resources are available for mental health outreach programs. Which of the following apply?**

    A. Grants from government or private sectors.
    B. Revenue generated from other mental health services
    C. Fund raising events
    D. All of the above

8. **To manage a counseling program effectively, a person must have _____ and _____.**

    A. Supervisory and administrative skills
    B. Patience and fortitude
    C. A secretary and financial administrator
    D. None of the above

9. **Program management involves _____ and _____.**

    A. Applying theories and techniques with personnel
    B. Integrating teaching and counseling skills
    C. Facilitating and planning events
    D. None of the above

10. **What are two ways a program manager can build rapport and collaborate with other agencies to help people in the community?**

    A. Sponsor a community event and invite other agencies to collaborate in planning and execution
    B. Attend community events and join committees focused on community goals
    C. Both A and B
    D. None of the above

11. **As a member of a multi-disciplinary team you might be expected to _____.**

    A. Chair a committee
    B. Organize an event
    C. Attend weekly meetings
    D. All of the above

12. **What is a multi-disciplinary team in reference to the field of counseling?**

    A. Groups of professionals in a variety of fields meeting for a particular purpose
    B. A team developed to provide disciplinary action for certain behavioral issues
    C. Parents and teachers meeting to assess student actions
    D. All of the above

13. **What would not be a focus of a multi-disciplinary team in the realm of mental health services?**

   A. Domestic violence
   B. Substance use in the community
   C. Traffic violations
   D. Teen pregnancy

14. **There is a state prison in your community. What type of community outreach might be needed in your area?**

   A. Support groups for partners of incarcerated adults
   B. Children of incarcerated parents outreach
   C. Both A and B
   D. No community outreach is needed in this area

15. **What type of therapy would be the basis for a smoking cessation program?**

   A. Adlerian therapy
   B. Existential therapy
   C. Cognitive behavior therapy
   D. Person-centered therapy

16. **Support groups are effective in what areas of concern?**

   A. Divorce
   B. Parenting a child with disabilities
   C. Grief
   D. All of the above

17. **Group work may not be effective for which type of disorder?**

   A. Depression
   B. Anxiety
   C. Eating disorders
   D. Autism Spectrum disorders

18. **Rational Emotive Behavioral Therapy (REBT) has been shown to work effectively for what type of concerns?**

   A. Mild to moderately severe mental health disorders
   B. Traumatic childhood concerns
   C. Psychotic disorders
   D. None of the above

19. **Solution-based brief therapy is ideal for _____.**

   A. Adjustment problems
   B. Anxiety and depression
   C. Both A and B
   D. Dissociative identity disorder

20. When considering treatment goals for brief solution-based therapy, what considerations need to be kept in mind?

    A. Goals should be written down
    B. Goals need to be meaningful and important to clients
    C. Goals need to be small and within easy reach
    D. All of the above

21. In multimodal therapy, the "D" in the seven areas of functioning acronym BASIC ID is for _____ .

    A. Desire
    B. Discipline
    C. Dancing
    D. Drugs

22. One of the goals in Developmental Counseling and Therapy (DCT) is _____ .

    A. To identify and restructure distorted thinking
    B. To change behavior
    C. To help people gain more integration, organization, flexibility, and range in their cognitive development structures.
    D. None of the above

23. In Developmental Counseling and Therapy (DCT), the sensorimotor environmental structuring is a process that _____ .

    A. Provides direction, promotes awareness, and focuses attention on the here and now
    B. Encourages cause and effect thinking, promoting a constructive action
    C. Promotes analysis, reflection, insight, and recognition of patterns
    D. Facilitates integration and thinking that generates multiple perspectives and promotes awareness of self.

24. How can a clinician gain self-knowledge to assist in finding their clinical approach?

    A. Through inventories such as the Myers-Briggs Type Indicator (MBTI)
    B. Feedback received from others
    C. Talking to their mothers
    D. Both A and B

25. Why are most of the questions on the MMPI test about abnormal behavior?

    A. Most clients have abnormal behavior
    B. Its purpose is to rule out the abnormal behaviors
    C. It is designed primarily to diagnose psychological disorders
    D. Both A and B

26. **What is the difference between the MMPI-1 and MMPI-2?**

   A. MMPI-1 is more up-to-date with current cultural and language changes
   B. MMPI-2 is a revision of the tests done in 1989
   C. Neither one has been changed much
   D. None of the above

27. **What is the Rorschach test?**

   A. A method for assessing personality
   B. It's a test known as the inkblot test
   C. It's a test using cards with pictures
   D. All of the above

28. **A test using cards that portray human figures in a variety of settings and situations is called_____.**

   A. The Thematic Apperception Test
   B. The Unconscious Personality Test
   C. The Apperception Test
   D. The Henry Murray Test

29. **What are two of the criticisms of projective tests?**

   A. Respondents cannot fake their responses; the tests are too easy
   B. The tests cause too much anxiety; they are too unstructured
   C. Two different examiners can interpret the same results two different ways; low reliability and validity of the tests
   D. The results are worthless; the tests take too much time

30. **_____ is the process of observing behavior as it is occurring.**

   A. Behavioral observation
   B. Systematic observation
   C. Scientific observation
   D. Information observation

31. **One way an expectancy table can be used in counseling is for making decisions. Another way is:**

   A. To provide clients with information on how long they can expect to be in counseling.
   B. To tell you when your baby is due.
   C. To provide clients with information on how they might succeed in a particular area.
   D. None of the above.

32. **When a client first starts counseling, it is imperative to:**

   A. Have reliable transportation.
   B. Have supportive surroundings.
   C. Post it on Facebook.
   D. All of the above.

33. **A main aspect of test development using the empirical approach is:**

A. Having the capability to maneuver through the obstacles of one's own life and the world, and how you interact in the world.
B. Having a support group.
C. The construction of comparison groups.
D. None of the above.

34. **A preliminary step in utilizing tests in counseling is:**

A. To let the expectations of the test be known.
B. To check the client's IQ.
C. To gather information about the client's work history.
D. Both A and B.

35. **Why should testing not be the sole source of collecting data about a client?**

A. Assembling information from a variety of means helps to create a broader comprehension of the client and his or her issues.
B. Collecting data by more than one means takes longer and will generate more income.
C. It is too difficult to decide which test to use for any given client.
D. Both B and C

36. **Do assessment practices stop once the counseling begins?**

A. Yes, assessment is a one-time process that is performed before counseling begins.
B. Yes, assessments are too difficult to score and any further testing attempts will confuse the process.
C. No, assessment is an ongoing process throughout counseling.
D. No, assessment takes place at the beginning of each session.

37. **Another reason to continue testing throughout the term of counseling is:**

A. to reassure the client that he or she is getting the most for his or her money.
B. Ongoing assessment will bring to light new needs that may have surfaced during counseling.
C. To confuse the client and make the client think he or she needs counseling even more than he or she actually does.
D. None of the above.

38. **How can role playing play a part in qualitative assessment?**

A. Role playing provides the counselor with insight into how the client behaves in a given situation.
B. Role playing can provide the client with an alternative way to handle a situation.
C. Role playing can aid in telling if acting will be a good career choice for the client.
D. Both A and B.

39. **In the counseling assessment process, who is responsible for obtaining or bringing forth information needed for successful counseling?**

A. The client
B. The counselor
C. The receptionist
D. The client's spouse

40. **What is integral therapy?**

A. A type of therapy that assesses the many intertwined parts of a client, including biological, cognitive, emotional, rational, and spiritual.
B. A type of therapy in which negative patterns of thinking about one's self and the world are challenged.
C. A type of therapy that focuses on altering a client's attitude, perceptions, and ways of thinking.
D. A type of therapy that looks into the past to attain forgotten, ignored, or repressed experiences that may be the cause of current problems.

41. **Which type of therapy was developed by Aaron T. Beck?**

A. Integral therapy
B. Depth therapy
C. Regression therapy
D. Cognitive therapy

42. **Is there a difference between regression therapy and psychodynamic therapy?**

A. No, they are both the same.
B. Yes, regression therapy is more solution-focused and psychodynamic therapy is more about the process and the experience of coming to a solution.
C. Yes, regression therapy is used more with adults whereas psychodynamic therapy is mainly associated with its use in treating adolescents.
D. None of the above.

43. What are some techniques used in psychodynamic therapy?

A. Self-empowerment and grounding.
B. Free association and building a strong therapeutic alliance.
C. Identifying and investigating automatic thoughts.
D. Interpersonal relationships between client and therapist and placing emphasis on current situations.

44. One of the goals of clients who engage in _____ therapy is to face their fears and overcome them through action.

A. Narrative
B. Collaborative
C. Existential
D. Psycho-physical

45. What type of problems is Motivational Enhancement Therapy mainly used to treat?

A. Relationship problems
B. Depression
C. Phobias
D. Addictions

46. A type of therapy that centers on the belief that knowledge is the result of social rhetoric and conversation is _____.

A. Collaborative therapy
B. Narrative therapy
C. Possibility therapy
D. Depth therapy

47. What is Schema therapy used to treat?

A. Addictions
B. Relationship problems
C. Eating disorders
D. None of the above

48. What is the main aspect of family therapy?

A. That many people who struggle with deep emotional issues are unable to express themselves verbally.
B. That a person must reflect on childhood memories he or she has and learn from them how to flourish in relationships.
C. That clients learn to separate themselves from their ideas and emotions and, instead, focus on what is presently going on in their minds and bodies.
D. It is dependent on the client's family to find answers to problems.

Career Development

1. Which of the following sets of descriptive words fit with the definition of Industrial/Organizational (I/O) psychology.

    A. Jobs, people, money
    B. Individual behavior, environment, organizational structure
    C. Formal, reverse, job related
    D. Machines, people, habits

2. Industrial/Organizational psychology is a combination of three major areas. They include:

    A. Human Factors and Organizational Psychology
    B. Personnel and Organizational Psychology
    C. Abnormal and Social Psychology
    D. Both A and B

3. What does Human Factor Psychology address?

    A. Human input into machines
    B. Machines/ tools
    C. Devices that produce a product or service
    D. All of the above

4. Personnel Psychology is obviously related with personnel. What would that include?

    A. Telephones, monitoring people
    B. Transportation, work hours
    C. Recruiting, selecting, training
    D. Giggles, coffee breaks

5. What does an employee performance evaluation tell a company?

    A. Both B and D
    B. Any concerns the employee may have
    C. How much time is being spent at the 'water cooler'
    D. Identifies training needs and present employee skill level

6. What two words best describe a Job Analysis?

    A. Recruitment, selection
    B. Description, tasks
    C. Structured, machines
    D. Relaxed, friendly

7. Sexual harassment is a big part of the work environment and takes place in the political and academic setting, as well as in the workplace. Which of the following choices is a true statement about sexual harassment?

    A. Older women who report are often ignored or ridiculed
    B. Younger, prettier women who report are often said to be asking for it
    C. Victims often face difficulties such as unemployment or demotions if they resistor report
    D. All of the above

8. Sexual harassment is primarily _____ and not an expression of sexual desire.

    A. An animal act
    B. A primitive act
    C. An act of stupidity
    D. An assertion and abuse of power

9. There have been two basic types of managers identified by their different assumptions about human nature. Pick their theories.

    A. Theory A -all employees spend too much time visiting
    B. Theory X - all employees dislike work and are lazy
    C. Theory Y- all employees like work and seek responsibility
    D. Both B and C

10. A key method of Theory Y management is the idea that the people involved in implementing a decision are also involved in making it. This is referred to as:

    A. Participative Decision Making
    B. Combination Decision Making
    C. Management Decision Making
    D. Employee Decision Making

11. Why do some workers put in long hours and stay late while some arrive late and leave early? These differences are why employers are interested in Worker Motivation. There are three Theories that promote worker motivation. Pick one of them as listed here.

    A. Working longer hours theory
    B. Equity theory
    C. Motivate theory
    D. Work balance theory

12.

The theory that a match between a person's personality and their work results in increased job satisfaction is known as _____.

    A. Theory Y
    B. Hawthorne Theory
    C. Trait and Factor Theory
    D. None of the above

13. **Part of Personnel Psychology includes interviewing. Most people hate being interviewed. One of the reasons for this is something called 'First date' syndrome. What is not associated with this syndrome?**

    A. Unstated outcome
    B. Behaving with artificial care/skill
    C. Not knowing how to interview
    D. None of the above

14. **Why are interviewees tense and anxious?**

    A. They know they are being evaluated and compared
    B. They usually don't know the interviewer
    C. They don't think they are good enough
    D. People are always nervous in new situations

15. **When one person meets another, impressions tend to be formed immediately. These first impressions are often difficult to change. What word, or words, is given to describe this situation?**

    A. First Meeting syndrome
    B. Subjectivity
    C. Impression syndrome
    D. None of the above

16. **There are some things that can help an interviewee be more prepared, and thus less nervous, for an interview. Which of the following is not one of these things?**

    A. Research job
    B. Role playing
    C. Being yourself
    D. Taking charge of interview

17. **Nearly all companies do employee evaluations at least every year. During the evaluation process, there is something referred to as the 'Halo Effect.' What does this refer to?**

    A. That the person named is perfect
    B. The person concerned is religious
    C. Tendency to rate people too high or too low on one outstanding trait
    D. Tendency to rate people based on the sum of all characteristics.

18. **Employee training typically begins with an orientation program. What is the major unstated goal of orientation?**

    A. Transmitting organizational culture
    B. Developing technical skills
    C. Learning where the break room is located
    D. None of the above

19. **A career counselor can help people develop the skills needed for effective job seeking. What are two of these skills?**

    A. Driving a car; telephone etiquette
    B. Resume writing; interview techniques
    C. Organization; hand writing
    D. Career counselors do not help people develop job seeking skills

20. **When meeting with a client, a career counselor might _____.**

    A. Have the client take an interest inventory
    B. Assist the client with self-exploration to determine goals
    C. Teach decision-making skills
    D. All of the above

21. **In the Social Cognitive Career theory, people sometimes eliminate many career possibilities when looking at choices because _____.**

    A. They have very narrow interests
    B. They have faulty self-efficacy beliefs
    C. They follow their parents' footsteps
    D. None of the above

22. **In Social Cognitive Career theory, counselors may need to assist a client in _____.**

    A. Analyzing career barrier perceptions
    B. Identifying closed occupational possibilities
    C. Both A and B
    D. None of the above

23. **In modifying faulty self-efficacy beliefs, a social cognitive career counselor may assist their client to _____ and _____.**

    A. Adjust their attitude and create new outcomes
    B. Develop new performance beliefs and reanalyze past experiences
    C. Regroup their skills and reorganize their resume
    D. None of the above

24. **What is the role of the Occupational Outlook Handbook in career counseling?**

    A. Paperweight
    B. Source of information about careers
    C. Evaluation tool
    D. None of the above

25.

Who created the Archway Model of Career Determinants theory?

    A. Erik Erikson
    B. James Joyce
    C. Donald Super
    D. Jean Piaget

26. **How many classifications are included in Holland's theory of Vocational Types?**

    A. Five
    B. Four
    C. Six
    D. Eight

27. **In Bandura's social cognitive theory, what is the meaning of self-efficacy?**

    A. It is a person's belief in their ability to organize and perform the actions required to produce a desired outcome
    B. It is the belief that all actions a person takes will be beneficial to one's self
    C. It is a theory that all people believe the best about themselves
    D. None of the above

28. **A person who scores highly in the Realistic area of Holland's vocational types is someone who_____.**

    A. Is very realistic in their goals.
    B. Enjoys helping others reach their goals
    C. Likes to work with their hands, machines, and tools.
    D. Has a down-to-earth approach to life

29. **What is the meaning of life roles as it applies to career counseling?**

    A. We take on a variety of roles in life as we age and this affects our career choices
    B. Life roles are how a person views one's self
    C. There are no "life roles" as it applies to career counseling
    D. Both A and B

30. **In Super's development of self-concept, one of the stages is exploration. What is the age range for this stage?**

    A. Birth to mid-teens
    B. Mid-teens to early twenties
    C. Early twenties to mid-thirties
    D. There is no stage of exploration in Super's theory

31. **What should be included in your career goal plan?**

    A. A timeframe for reaching your career goals
    B. How many children you expect to have
    C. How many hours a week you can devote for charity work
    D. Both A and C

32. **Studies that have examined counselors' skills have found that the most under-skilled counselors tend to:**

    A. Charge the most for their services.
    B. Target poorer clients.
    C. Be the most likely to overestimate their performances.
    D. Spend the most money on advertising.

33. **Employment options for counselors include starting their own practices, joining an established practice, and _____.**

    A. Working in an academic setting.
    B. Working in a hospital prescribing medication.
    C. Working in a pharmacy.
    D. All of the above.

34. **What are some negative factors counselors may face when beginning their careers?**

    A. Incompetence
    B. Licensing and credentialing
    C. Ethical and legal concerns
    D. All of the above

35. **Some personal concerns a new counselor may face are:**

    A. Advertising and client recruiting.
    B. Having the correct work attire and office furnishings.
    C. The need for recognition and balancing personal and professional life.
    D. None of the above.

36. **What is one question a counselor must consider when deciding how to continue his or her career path?**

    A. Do I have enough money to purchase a vacation home?
    B. Am I meeting enough people through this line of work?
    C. What will my peers think of me if I change careers?
    D. Is this the right environment for me?

37. **What is a common problem veteran counselors may have if they remain in an academic setting?**

    A. They miss out on careers in other areas.
    B. They may not be able to relate to their students due to the age difference.
    C. They may rise to a supervisory position too quickly.
    D. Both A and C

38. **If a counselor cannot find professional support and helpful resources, a lack of _____ may result.**

    A. Morals
    B. Commitment
    C. Ethics
    D. Control

39. **What can make a counselor want to remain in the same job for an extended period?**

    A. Having clients who are continuously depressed.
    B. Having a nice secretary.
    C. Having clients who are mandated to obtain counseling.
    D. Development of a career ladder listing attainable promotions within the company.

40. **What will help promote professional development within a company?**

    A. Micromanagement of the company.
    B. Promoting involvement at the local, regional, and national levels.
    C. Restricting personal relationships between colleagues
    D. Reporting unethical behavior.

41. **How can supporting flexible schedules help a company maintain a low turnover rate among counselors?**

    A. It will allow the counselor to sleep in each morning.
    B. It will allow counselors the time needed to seek other employment.
    C. There will be times when no counselors are available, thus cutting back on overhead.
    D. It will allow counselors the freedom to attend to the needs of their families.

42. **Why is it advisable to have a plan in mind for the next five or ten years?**

    A. So you will always have a goal toward which to work
    B. So you can stop working once you have reached your goal
    C. So you can stop working at any time
    D. None of the above

43. **What are some ways you can further your professional career?**

    A. In-house or external training
    B. Conferences and workshops
    C. Work-based research
    D. All of the above

44. **Keeping up with _____ can help you further your career.**

    A. The latest pop-culture news
    B. Technology
    C. Stock prices
    D. Your friends and family

45. **Building and maintaining a _____ will be invaluable as the role of the counselor changes.**

    A. Social network
    B. Professional network
    C. Social calendar
    D. Web page

46. **A good counselor will take notice of _____ in the economy and in his or her profession.**

    A. Profits and losses
    B. Stocks and bonds
    C. Changes and trends
    D. Both A & B

47. **It is important for you to _____ consistent with your career goals.**

    A. See that your portfolio is
    B. Bring in income
    C. Build a reputation
    D. Make money that is

48. **Who said, "You can't build a reputation on what you say you are going to do"?**

    A. President Obama
    B. Henry Ford
    C. Derek Jeter
    D. Charles Schultz

49. **Good _____ and _____ are imperative for successful counselors.**

    A. Hygiene and fashion sense
    B. Learning and information skills
    C. Reflexes and stamina
    D. Focusing and attention span

Professional and Ethical Issues

1. **Which of the following options most closely constitutes incompetent practice?**

    A. Practicing in an area in which one has not completed adequate training
    B. Working with a physical disability
    C. Knowing a client's ethnicity
    D. All of the above

2. **What method is often used in securing informed consent?**

    A. Finger print document
    B. Written consent
    C. Oral consent
    D. Both B and C

3. **How would you describe a dual relationship in one word?**

    A. Ethical
    B. Unethical
    C. Depends
    D. Nice

4. **Counseling practitioners may fully discuss clients with which of the following?**

    A. Their mothers
    B. Other counselors in the coffee room
    C. The client's mother
    D. None of the above

5. **What ethical issues are related to the research process?**

    A. Plagiarism
    B. Humane animal care and use
    C. Institutional approval
    D. All of the above

6. **What rights do clients have in relation to the testing process?**

    A. No special 'rights'
    B. Just to know when a test is being given and the scores
    C. Informed consent, signed release for any information given to others
    D. The right to payment for participation

7. **What are some of the ethics and laws governing school counselors?**

    A. School counselors are released from most counseling ethics/laws
    B. Same as all counseling ethics, plus there is a special book on ethics/laws for school counselors
    C. There is an American School Counselor Association to help school counselors
    D. Both B and C

8. **Are there any special considerations needed for divorce and custody litigation?**

    A. Keeping the adults focused on what is best for the children
    B. Dealing with the stress for each and all family members
    C. Give the kids to the Mom, she's used to dealing with them
    D. Both A and B

9. **According to the preamble of "Ethical Principles of Psychologists" published by the American Psychology Association, what are some goals psychologists can use to guide their continuing practice of psychology?**

    A. To maintain psychologist's competence
    B. To preserve the dignity and best interests of clients
    C. To serve the best interests of colleagues, students and research participants
    D. All of the above

10. **In the beginnings of psychology there were eight schools of thought, each one differing in the method of treatment. These eight included:**

    A. Functionalism, Introspection, Behaviorism
    B. Structuralism, Behaviorism, Sensationalism
    C. Gestalt, Psychobiology, Humanistic
    D. Hypothesism, Experimentalism, Structuralism

11. **Structuralism was one of the earliest schools. What was the focus or theory of that school?**

    A. Focused on the basic sensations and feelings of experiences
    B. Focused on the study of mental processes
    C. Focused on touchy, feely things
    D. Both A and B

12. **How has the history of psychology and all its many methods affected the psychology methods or practices we use today?**

    A. Very much; we use a little from many of the older schools
    B. Not at all; we use very little or none of the old school ways
    C. Psychology didn't even really start until the 1980's
    D. None of the above

13. **Sigmund Freud's theory is still controversial and receives a lot of criticism. Why?**

   A. Much of his theory had no basis for belief
   B. Its base is individual case studies without a control of 'normal' people
   C. His concepts and techniques are difficult to study scientifically
   D. All of the above

14. **Some of the degrees available in psychology are as follows:**

   A. MA, MS, DMT
   B. DMFT, PhD, PsyD
   C. PHD, LPsy, HIT
   D. Both A and C

15. **Professional licenses for Master degrees include:**

   A. LMFT, CRC, LPC
   B. LPC-BE, FGA, ABC
   C. LCSW, LPC, LMHC
   D. Both A and C

16. **Do licensing and degrees differ from state to state?**

   A. No; they are standard across the board
   B. Yes; each state has its own requirements
   C. The APA controls all licensure and degree requirements
   D. You don't need either a degree or license, just go for it

17. **Who is Victor Frankl?**

   A. The father of psychotherapy
   B. A developmental theorist
   C. An actor
   D. An early existentialist therapist

18. **According to Gestalt therapists, people experience psychological difficulties because _____.**

   A. They have become cut off from important parts of themselves
   B. They do not eat a balanced diet
   C. They had parents who ignored them
   D. All of the above

19. **In order to supervise other counselors in their clinical work, a clinician must have _____.**

   A. 1000 hours of client interaction
   B. 3000 hours of client interaction
   C. Specific credentials that vary from state to state
   D. Five years of experience

20. **What is diversity training?**

    A. Training on which type of therapeutic intervention to use
    B. How to work with different age groups
    C. Training on different cultures, ethnicity, experiences
    D. B and C

21. **A Latina counselor agrees to work with a client from an Asian background. What does this counselor need to effectively assist her client?**

    A. Diversity training
    B. A degree in Asian Culture
    C. A recommendation from another therapist
    D. An eagerness to assist the client

22. **How often does a clinical supervisor need to meet with the counselors he/she is supervising?**

    A. Once a week
    B. Every day
    C. Monthly
    D. Time varies state to state

23. **When a counselor is seeing clients under supervision, what does the client need to know about the arrangement?**

    A. How often the counselor meets with the supervisor
    B. That the counselor is being supervised and will be consulting with a licensed clinician to discuss clients status
    C. The client does not need to know the counselor is being supervised
    D. Both A and B

24. **A lead clinician might provide in-service training for counselors under his supervision. What types of training might be provided?**

    A. Stress management techniques
    B. Group facilitation
    C. Wine tasting
    D. A and B

25. **In diversity, or cultural awareness training, what subjects might be taught?**

    A. Types of food each culture prefers
    B. Belief systems
    C. Geographic location of cultures of origin
    D. None of the above

26. **The lead clinician notices several of the counselors within the organization are using EMDR (Eye Movement Desensitization and Reprocessing) in their work with clients. She is curious about whether this is an effective method. What can she do?**

    A. Perform a data analysis of research in EMDR
    B. Read a bunch of articles
    C. Take an EMDR training class
    D. Nothing. She is very busy and the clients seem to be doing well.

27. **Evaluating the performance of other counselors is an important aspect of supervision. What is an appropriate way to evaluate another counselor?**

    A. Ask the counselor's clients what they think of him/her
    B. Sit in on a session or videotape the session (with client permission)
    C. Review client files for accuracy of paperwork and documented client progress
    D. Both B and C

28. **What is quality assurance and control as it pertains to a clinical practice?**

    A. It has to do with the air quality within the building
    B. Assuring the clients that the counselors are of good quality
    C. Ensuring all client files are accurate and up-to-date
    D. All of the above

29. **When performing an evaluation on another counselor, a supervisor will look at what areas of performance?**

    A. Time management skills
    B. Accurate and timely paperwork completion
    C. Progression toward client goals
    D. All of the above

30. **A counselor is having a difficult time making progress with a client toward the goals initially determined in the treatment plan. What are some options available to rectify this concern?**

    A. Consultation with other counselors in the practice
    B. Terminate working with the client
    C. Asking another counselor to sit in on a session (with client permission)
    D. A and C

31. **A clinic is seeing an increase in people with a Major Depressive Disorder diagnosis. What might the lead clinician do about this?**

    A. Nothing; these disorders tend to be cyclic
    B. Provide refresher training on accurate diagnosis and treatment for MDD
    C. Bring this to the notice of other clinicians in the weekly meeting
    D. Both B and C

32. **What is a community needs assessment?**

   A. Assessing the variety of jobs that need filling in the community
   B. Gathering information about a community regarding strengths, resources, and areas for improvement
   C. Communities don't need assessment, people do!
   D. A and C

33. **Why would a director of a counseling practice conduct a community needs assessment?**

   A. Curiosity
   B. To match clinic services with community needs
   C. To assist with the health and well-being of the community
   D. B and C

34. **A population within a clinic's service area is not accessing mental health services, even when it is determined there is a need. An informal assessment reveals they do not have reliable transportation. What is one option to remedy this concern?**

   A. A satellite office in that area
   B. An outreach program in the area
   C. Ignore it
   D. A and B

35. **The lead clinician often determines which counselors see new clients. What factors determine placement?**

   A. Counselor's area of expertise; matched to presenting problem
   B. Age and gender of client
   C. Caseload of counselor
   D. All of the above

36. **Professional ethics require a counselor to avoid dual relationships. What is a 'dual relationship'?**

   A. A concurrent relationship with a client
   B. Seeing more than one client in the same family
   C. Seeing a client who is also your accountant
   D. Both A and C

37. **What are the demographic characteristics of the effective clinician?**

   A. Age and gender
   B. Professional discipline (e.g., psychology, counseling, social work)
   C. No one knows exactly what makes an effective clinician.
   D. Both A and B

38. **Confidentiality is an important aspect of the therapeutic relationship. Why?**

    A. It helps clients feel safe in treatment
    B. It encourages clients to share material that might be painful or embarrassing
    C. It helps clinicians trust the client
    D. Both A and B

39.

Counselors have a responsibility to protect clients who threaten suicide or any other form of physical harm against themselves. This is usually called _____.

    A. Responsible reporting
    B. Duty to warn
    C. Duty to respond to threats
    D. Breaking confidentiality

40. **Some personal characteristics of an effective clinician are listed below. Which of the following is not one?**

    A. Friendly and likeable
    B. Realistic self-confidence and self-esteem
    C. Affirm rather than diminish others
    D. Active social life

41. **Clinicians tend to choose counseling approaches that are _____ their personality styles.**

    A. Opposite of
    B. Unrelated to
    C. Compatible with
    D. None of the above

42. **There is a high level of substance use in teens within your practice area. What might be developed to address this concern?**

    A. Public awareness campaign against drug and alcohol use
    B. A teen support group
    C. A series of parenting classes addressing teen behavior
    D. All of the above

43. **When acting as a consultant to another counselor, what skills might be the most helpful?**

    A. Active listening skills
    B. Organization skills
    C. Time management skills
    D. Relaxation skills

44. How do ethics and values differ?

A. Ethics dictate the boundaries of professional therapy, whereas values predict the stimulus and workings of therapy.
B. Ethics predict the stimulus and workings of therapy, whereas values dictate the boundaries of professional therapy.
C. Ethics can be adapted to a given situation, whereas values cannot.
D. There is no difference.

45. If a counselor is aware that a client is engaging in using illegal drugs, is the counselor bound by law to notify the proper authorities of this activity?

A. No, the counselor should try to get in on the action.
B. No, the only way the counselor should break confidentiality is if the client's activities will likely do harm to himself or herself, another person, or property.
C. Yes, any illegal activity should be reported to the proper authorities.
D. Yes, but it should only be done anonymously so as not to lose the trust of the client.

46. What are some issues every counselor must consider before making an ethical decision?

A. The makeup of the counselor's community
B. The makeup of the client's community
C. The client's culture
D. All of the above

47. Is it important for a counselor to question him or herself as much, if not more, than he or she questions other counselors?

A. No, if a counselor begins to question him or herself, this doubt will eventually become apparent to the client.
B. No, a counselor should always question his peers and take steps to correct them.
C. Yes, questioning one's self is positive and productive, and will challenge the counselor to explore new avenues.
D. None of the above.

48. Ethical alertness is an ongoing, progressive procedure that involves _____ and _____.

A. Continual questioning and personal responsibility.
B. Continuing education and paying dues.
C. Building a practice and having more income.
D. Watching peers and turning them in for ethical violations.

Fundamentals

1.

The classification system developed by a task force of the American Psychiatric Association is _____.

    A. The DRCI-V
    B. The MMCD-IV
    C. The DMS-II
    D. The DSM-5

2.

Does the DSM-5 explain the causes of disorders?

    A. No
    B. Yes
    C. A few
    D. That's what it's for

3.

The first edition of the DSM was published in 1952. When was the last edition, DSM-5, originally issued?

    A. 1879
    B. 1994
    C. 2001
    D. 2013

4.

Why do the creators of the DSM keep releasing new editions of the manual?

    A. To incorporate new information
    B. To incorporate changes in the way abnormal behaviors are viewed
    C. To change the descriptions and categories
    D. All of the above

5.

Does the DSM-5 classify people?

    A. Yes, according to their disorders
    B. Absolutely not
    C. You would think so
    D. Can't say, never have looked at it

6. What about the term "insanity"? Where does it fit in?

A. It is a legal term
B. It is an exception
C. It is an action word
D. It is a loosely used word with no legal meaning

7.

A revised version of the DSM-IV, titled the DSM-IV-TR, was published in July 2000, with a new edition printed in 2013, the DSM-5. True or False?

A. True
B. False

8. Which client characteristic seems unrelated to outcome?

A. Intelligence
B. Age
C. Education
D. Socioeconomic level

9. Elena's client admitted to drinking excessively at a party. Which of the following questions is most likely to have a negative impact on the client?

A. How did you feel about that?
B. What happened?
C. What would you do differently next time?
D. Why did you drink so much?

10. Clients with which of the following disorders are most likely to lack the ability to engage in the self-examination required by Adlerian therapy?

A. Impulse control disorders
B. Psychotic disorders
C. Personality disorders
D. Anxiety disorders

11. Which of the following is not an open question?

A. What brought you here?
B. How are things going?
C. Did you have a good week?
D. How did you react?

12. People most likely to enjoy the energetic and interactive approach of REBT are those with which characteristics?

    A. Low self-esteem
    B. Highly motivated, pragmatic, logical
    C. Fairly resilient, tough minded
    D. B and C

13. A clinician can create a therapeutic alliance with their client by _____.

    A. Mutuality
    B. Genuineness
    C. Hope
    D. All of the above

14. There are five types of psychotherapeutic alliances. Which type focuses on shared goals and an agreement to engage in certain tasks to achieve those goals?

    A. Transpersonal relationships
    B. I-You relationships
    C. Working alliances
    D. Reparative/developmentally needed relationships

15. One aspect of role induction is _____.

    A. Listening to the client
    B. Familiarizing the client with the nature of counseling
    C. Ensuring the room is set up properly
    D. None of the above

16. Duty to warn is an important part of professional ethics in therapy. What is not an aspect of duty to warn?

    A. Duty to protect others who are endangered by a client
    B. Duty to protect clients who threaten suicide or other forms of physical harm
    C. Duty to seek consultation from a colleague or supervisor when faced with an issue to break confidentiality
    D. Duty to warn a client when the therapist will be on vacation

17. Two personal characteristics of the effective clinician are _____.

    A. Friendly and likeable
    B. Patient and inflexible
    C. Motivated by money and high self-esteem
    D. Humorous and loud

18. **A critical component of the diagnostic interview includes which of the following?**

A. Family and social history
B. Medical history
C. Previous diagnoses
D. All of the above

19. **When do clinicians need to refer clients to other professionals?**

A. When a possible underlying medical condition is discovered
B. When additional concerns discovered are not within the clinician's expertise
C. When the clinician is having a bad day
D. A and B

20. **Global Assessment of Functioning is a numerical scale (0-100) that clinicians use to subjectively assess the social, occupational, and psychological functioning of adults. Which is not a part of the scale?**

A. **100-91:** Superior functioning in a wide range of activities; life's problems never seem to get out of hand; is sought out by others because of his/her many positive qualities. No symptoms.
B. **10-1:** Persistent danger of severely hurting self or others (e.g., recurrent violence); persistent inability to maintain minimal personal hygiene; serious suicidal act with clear expectation of death.
C. **80-71:** If symptoms are present, they are transient and expectable reactions to psycho-social stressors (e.g., difficulty concentrating after family argument); no more than slight impairment in social, occupational, or school functioning (e.g., temporarily falling behind in schoolwork).
D. All of the above are part of the GAF

21. **When assessing a client's progress toward counseling goals, a clinician should _____.**

A. Ask the client how they are doing
B. Refer to the treatment plan
C. Ask other clinicians how they think the client is doing
D. Not worry about assessing progress; it's all about the journey

22. **Many tests are available to assess client functioning. What is a reliable, valid test for assessing depression?**

A. The MMPI-TM2
B. The QOLI
C. The HTP
D. The BDI

23. **The MBHI, or Million Behavioral Health Inventory, instrument is a brief self-report personality inventory designed to help the clinician assess the psychological coping factors related to the physical health care of adult medical patients. It is useful in:**

A. Evaluation and screening of physically ill, injured, and surgical patients
B. Workers' compensation evaluations to help assess stress-related claims
C. Evaluation and screening of individuals in specialty clinics or programs (e.g., pain, stress, headache)
D. All of the above

24. **One of the reasons bipolar disorder can be difficult to diagnose in a child under ten is that _____.**

A. The symptoms mimic or overlap ADHD
B. Children under ten do not experience bipolar disorder
C. Children under ten usually are very irritable anyway
D. None of the above

25. **Common factors in effective treatment are _____.**

A. Acquiring insight and new understanding
B. Developing new perceptions or views of one's stressors or problems
C. Enjoying the process of counseling
D. Both A and B

26. **In Brief Solution-Based therapy, the underlying theory is _____.**

A. Problems stem from the inability of the ego to suppress or moderate drives from the id.
B. A climate of acceptance and unconditional positive regard promotes self-esteem and facilitates client growth
C. Small behavioral changes lead to larger changes that have ripple effects on the whole system
D. People are self-determining and choose everything, including their thoughts, actions, and emotions.

27.

The Diagnostic and Statistical Manual of Mental Disorders Text-revised, 5th Edition (DSM-5) is utilized by professionals to diagnose psychiatric disorders. Unlike previous versions of the DSM, it does not use a multi-axis model for diagnosis. Which DSM-IV-TR axis had its criteria modified and included in the DSM-5, but not in the list of disorders?

A. Axis I
B. Axis II
C. Axis IV
D. Axis V

28.

Which of the following is not a Cluster B personality disorder?

> A. Antisocial Personality Disorder
> B. Borderline Personality Disorder
> C. Narcissistic Personality Disorder
> D. All of the above are Cluster B personality disorders

29.

The DSM-5 includes a section for significant psychosocial and environmental problems. Which of the following would you report in this section?

> A. Recent job loss
> B. Failing the GED exam
> C. Difficulty finding housing
> D. All of the above

30. **When using the Global Assessment of Functioning (GAF) scale, clinicians need to start _____.**

> A. At the bottom and evaluate each range for the function of the individual
> B. At the top level and keep moving down the scale until the best match is found
> C. By guessing at about which level the person might be functioning
> D. With another type of assessment altogether

31.

What is the differential diagnosis for Reactive Attachment Disorder according to the DSM-5?

> A. Schizophrenia
> B. Depression
> C. Pervasive Developmental Disorders
> D. Anxiety Disorders

32. **A client states "It doesn't matter what I do, nothing goes right for me." This is an example of_____ in cognitive therapy.**

> A. All-or-nothing thinking
> B. Overgeneralization
> C. Catastrophizing
> D. Disqualifying the positive

33. **There are several techniques cognitive therapists use to elicit new cognitions in their clients. One of these techniques involves _____.**

  A. Going snow-skiing
  B. Jumping out of an airplane
  C. Activity scheduling
  D. Lying down when having troubling thoughts

34. **Self-talk is a technique in which people repeat to themselves positive and encouraging phrases that they have identified as helpful many times a day. This technique is used in _____ therapy.**

  A. Brief Psychodynamic therapy
  B. Cognitive therapy
  C. Jungian analytical therapy
  D. This is not a technique used in therapy

35. **What is the primary purpose of a strengths-based assessment?**

  A. To focus on the strengths of the client in all aspects of a client's life
  B. To find a meaning to struggling
  C. To create an awareness of how much the client has been through
  D. To assist in choosing a method of treatment

36. **Stress Inoculation Training (SIT) is a part of cognitive behavioral treatment. The therapist seeks to "immunize" a client from the adverse impact of stress by helping them successfully handle increasing levels of stress. There are three phases to this training. The first phase is _____.**

  A. Problem identification
  B. Conceptualization
  C. Development of skills
  D. Application and follow through

37. **When using *anchoring* in treatment with a client, the clinician is attempting to create _____.**

  A. A way to hold the client in his chair
  B. Planned positive responses to certain situations
  C. A metaphor for sailing
  D. Thought stopping procedures

38. **Cognitive therapy is based on the finding that changes in _____ lead to changes in _____.**

  A. Stress levels; the ability to sleep
  B. Hormones; thoughts
  C. Thinking; feeling and acting
  D. Believing; doing

39. **Research has shown there are several characteristics of a successful client. Two of these characteristics are _____ and _____.**

    A. Maturity and the capacity for relationships
    B. Intelligence and trustworthiness
    C. Sense of humor and adventure
    D. Trusting and giving

40. **Three essential skills needed for a clinician are _____, _____, and _____.**

    A. Organizational skills, listening skills, and patience
    B. The ability to structure time, team work, and clarity
    C. Time management skills, being alert, and able to clean
    D. Having respect for the client, encouraging optimism in seeking a realistic solution, and excellent communication skills.

41.

To make a diagnosis of a Major Depressive Episode based on DSM-5 criteria, a client would need to have five or more specific symptoms, with at least one of two necessary symptoms. Which symptom below is one of those necessary symptoms?

    A. Significant weight loss
    B. Feelings of worthlessness
    C. Markedly diminished interest or pleasure
    D. Fatigue or loss of energy

42. **What mental health diagnosis is most prevalent in children under age ten?**

    A. Obsessive-Compulsive Disorder (OCD)
    B. Attention Deficit/Hyperactivity Disorder (ADHD)
    C. Oppositional Defiant Disorder (ODD)
    D. Major Depressive Disorder (MDD)

43. **In couples therapy, the Dyadic Trust Scale _____.**

    A. Is an eight-item questionnaire
    B. Takes less than 3 minutes to take
    C. Focuses on trust between marriage partners
    D. All of the above

44. **In single parent families created by divorce, stressors for custodial parents include ____.**

    A. Finances
    B. Social
    C. Parenting alone
    D. All of the above

45. **Elderly couples are concerned about which of the following?**

    A. Finances
    B. Physical health
    C. Memory loss
    D. All of the above

46. **One task of a new couple according to Carter and McGoldrick is to _____.**

    A. Develop personal autonomy
    B. Learn to share with partner
    C. Develop a support group
    D. Adjust to decreased energy

47. **'Informed Consent' in a counseling situations means_____.**

    A. The clinician informs the client they will meet with them each week
    B. Outlines the clinician's responsibilities to the client
    C. Outlines the client's responsibilities to the clinician
    D. Both B and C

48. **The process of terminating psychotherapy or counseling with a client typically occurs in one of three ways: Clinician's choice, client's choice or by mutual agreement. Why would a clinician terminate working with the client?**

    A. They are tired of working with the client
    B. The clinician is experiencing life changes
    C. They do not think the client is making progress
    D. Clinician's do not terminate counseling with a client

49. **What does it usually mean when a clinician and client mutually agree to terminate treatment?**

    A. The client has made sufficient progress toward their goals
    B. The client no longer is enjoying treatment
    C. The clinician no longer wants to work with the client
    D. None of the above

Group Work

1. **In referring to group behavior, what is a 'norm'?**

    A. The person that acts out the most
    B. An expected behavior
    C. The group's behavior on a whole
    D. An unexpected behavior

2. **Conforming to group pressure out of a need for acceptance and approval is called _____.**

    A. Norm Fruitation
    B. Norm Conformation
    C. Normative Social Influence
    D. Normalization

3. **Every culture has definite 'norms.' One that seems to include all cultures has to do with maintaining an appropriate distance between people. This distance is referred to as _____.**

    A. Physical Space
    B. Interpersonal Distance
    C. Appropriate Distance
    D. Personal Space

4. **Groups seem to have several influences on an individual; one such influence comes from the need for direction and information and the belief that the group has more knowledge than the individual. This is referred to as _____.**

    A. Informational Social Influence
    B. Individual Need Influence
    C. Group Influence Need
    D. None of the above

5. **Attractive actors/actresses and popular sports stars are paid lots of money to endorse certain products because advertisers know that a majority of people want to be as cool, beautiful, or popular as they are. What is this major factor in conformity called?**

    A. Star Quality Groups
    B. Reference Groups
    C. Sky High Groups
    D. Attractiveness Factor

6. **What are the two major forms of social influence?**

    A. Imitation, Acceptance
    B. Personal, Approval
    C. Conformity, Obedience
    D. Information, Responsibility

7. One of the best ways to decrease destructive forms of obedience is by the assignment of _____.

    A. Approval
    B. Imitation
    C. Obedience
    D. Responsibility

8. What is conformity?

    A. Going along with the group
    B. Changing one's behavior because of real or imagined group pressure
    C. Doing what is popular at the time
    D. All of the above

9. How do you decide someone's motive for doing something? It has been found that most people first try to figure out if the person acted as a result of internal or external causes. Harold Kelly gave three criteria for answering the internal-external question; which two of them are listed below?

    A. Consistency, fault
    B. Mind-set, distinctiveness
    C. Unusual, consensus
    D. Consistency, consensus

10. There is a saliency bias associated with attribution. Which statement below most closely describes the meaning?

    A. Some personalities/behaviors are more noticeable than situational factors
    B. Some people just look/act guilty, so you recognize that
    C. It's a kind of cause/effect behavior
    D. There's no such thing

11. Why are people likely to blame the victim?

    A. It's an easy solution
    B. They don't take time to consider the true facts
    C. It helps us maintain our belief of bad things happen to bad people
    D. All of the above

12. Fear induction is one of the most effective persuasion techniques and is commonly used in advertisements and public service announcements. For fear tactics to work there must be three factors to the message. They are _____, _____, and _____.

A. Make the message dramatic, with lots of blood, then give it a happy ending
B. Show a really frightful situation, make it dramatic, then dissolve the fear
C. Must engender a lot of fear, audience must believe the message, instructions for avoiding the danger must be present
D. Listen to any "good" politician and you'll soon figure it out!

13. Are some people easier to persuade than others? Are you? There have been four major audience characteristics that have been studied in relation to persuasion, pick the one that is NOT a factor in this study.

A. Reactance
B. Personality Traits
C. Involvement
D. Resistance

14. Group practices of prejudice and discrimination have been a large part of our society. What is the meaning of in-group favoritism and out-group negativity?

A. An in-group tends to see themselves as more attractive, while an out-group is looked down upon
B. in-group is one to belong to, out-group consists of everybody outside the In-group
C. People create in-groups and out-groups by favoring one type of people over another
D. All of the above

15. A very dangerous kind of cognitive bias is the tendency to see more diversity among members of your 'in-group' and less diversity among the 'out-group'. This "they all look alike to me" tendency is termed the _____.

A. Out-group Are All Alike Effect
B. Out-group Homogeneity Effect
C. Out-group Are-As-One Effect
D. Out-group Personality Needs Effect

16. **When lower-class groups tend to blame each other rather than the upper class or the class system itself, it is known as Displaced Aggression. What causes this aggression to be displaced?**

    A. The source is too big to fight
    B. The source is capable of retaliating
    C. People often displace their aggression on a nonthreatening target
    D. All of the above

17. **Researchers have identified three methods to combat prejudice and aggression between groups. Which of the following choices is one of these methods?**

    A. Decreased contact
    B. Separate territories
    C. Super ordinate goals
    D. Displaced aggression

18. **What is the difference between prejudice and discrimination?**

    A. Nothing, they are used interchangeably
    B. Prejudice is an attitude, discrimination is negative behavior
    C. Discrimination often results from prejudice
    D. Both B and C

19. **How do prejudice and discrimination originate? Why do they persist? There are five major factors that are the most commonly cited sources of prejudice. Which pair of factors listed below are both factors that lead to prejudice?**

    A. Learning, individual personality needs
    B. Cognitive processes, aggression
    C. Economic /political competition, direct experiences
    D. Displaced aggression, competition

20. **Group therapy takes on three basic forms: Family Therapy, Support Groups, and _____.**

    A. Mental Health Groups
    B. Evaluation Groups
    C. Encounter Groups
    D. None of the above

21. **One of the types of therapy under the heading of family therapy is family systems therapy. Which sentence best describes this form of family therapy?**

    A. The family is seen as an interrelated system in which each member has a major role.
    B. Each member typically has comparable problems.
    C. By playing and observing different roles in relationships, people gain insight.
    D. Some families have more problems than others.

22. **What is the object of family therapy?**

    A. To have a fun family gathering
    B. Restore family relationships
    C. Bring out all the faulty family dynamics
    D. Intense family confrontations

23. **Support Groups are one of the best known of all group therapies. The most helpful factors of support groups can be:**

    A. The focus is not always on you
    B. Being with others that have similar problems can help us realize we're not alone
    C. Seeing others improve can be a source of hope and motivation
    D. All of the above

24. **What is a reason to join a support group?**

    A. A good way to meet your future mate
    B. I just need to get out of the house
    C. Self destructive behaviors, life crises
    D. Any of the above will do

25. **Encounter groups are designed to promote personal growth and interpersonal communication. By what means do they accomplish this?**

    A. They encourage participants to openly share emotion
    B. They encourage participants to tell it like it is to each other
    C. They encourage participants to have intense confrontations
    D. All of the above

26. **What is the biggest potential problem with group therapy?**

    A. You may not like your group
    B. The group leader may not be well trained/experienced enough
    C. There may not be enough 'breaks'
    D. None of the above

27. **What could be a most helpful aspect of group therapy?**

    A. Hearing others' problems
    B. Seeing others' reactions to the problems or situations
    C. Hearing similar comments from several group members concerning your problem or behavior
    D. There aren't any helpful aspects

28. **What is meant by 'roles in groups'?**

    A. Parts in a group play
    B. A set of behavioral patterns
    C. A category of people
    D. B and C

29. **What would a role garnered by informal learning and inference be?**

   A. A teacher or trainer
   B. A father or mother
   C. A clown or trapeze artist
   D. None of the above

30. **Do roles affect behavior?**

   A. Very much
   B. Not much
   C. A small amount
   D. Never

31. **What is "deindividuation"?**

   A. Taking out your aggressions
   B. Reinventing yourself
   C. Temporarily suspending your normal identity
   D. Going completely berserk

32. **When a group of people make decisions simply because they want to agree, it is called_____.**

   A. Stupidity
   B. Synchronization
   C. Mind guard
   D. Groupthink

33.

Group polarization generally occurs when a group decision becomes_____.

   A. Less reliable
   B. Less coherent
   C. More reliable
   D. More conservative or more risky

34. **How many people does it take to define a 'group'?**

   A. At least six
   B. Three or four
   C. Two or more
   D. At least ten

35. **_____ is one of the many kinds of support that groups offer to those who are grieving the loss of a loved one.**

   A. Peer-to-peer support
   B. Counseling referrals
   C. Survivor seminars
   D. All of the above

36. **Which of the following are reasons for group counseling in the grieving process?**

A. To help a person realize he is not alone; to give a person the opportunity to learn from others
B. To help a person socialize; to help a person make new friends
C. To give a person something else to think about; to help a person plan activities
D. To give a person something to do besides grieve

37. **Besides those groups supporting spousal loss, what might be another special loss group?**

A. For those who've lost an animal
B. For those recovering after a large financial loss
C. For those who have experienced the loss of a child
D. There are many groups

38. **Sometimes groups are facilitated by a trained professional; others are composed of _____.**

A. Only peers
B. Four or five counselors
C. The funeral director
D. Anyone willing to do it

39. **In group work, the _____ and _____ from both the clinician and the group members can accelerate the process of awareness and empowerment.**

A. Attention and interaction
B. Feedback and support
C. Knowledge and humor
D. Love and comfort

40. **Fritz Perls's work at the Esalen Institute emphasized the use of the _____ in a group setting.**

A. Talking Stick
B. Rotten Egg
C. Hot Seat
D. Empty Chair

41. **Making the Rounds is a Gestalt Therapy technique used in group settings. It is used in conjunction with the Hot Seat. In making the rounds, the group members _____.**

A. Say hi to the person sitting next to them on the hot seat
B. Listen to the person sitting in the hot seat say something about them
C. Focus on the person sitting in the hot seat and offer comments about that person
D. None of the above

42. **Rational Emotive Behavior Therapy (REBT) is particularly well-suited for treatment in a group setting, which offers participants the opportunity to _____ and _____ _____, as well as share feedback and reactions.**

    A. Watch and listen to others
    B. Observe and try out behaviors
    C. Lead others and role play
    D. Demonstrate skills and communicate feelings

43. **Because of its forceful and directive nature and its emphasis on client responsibility, Rational Emotive Behavior Therapy (REBT) is not appropriate for group work for people _____.**

    A. Who have psychotic disorders
    B. Who are highly suicidal or fragile
    C. Both A and B
    D. Who are highly confident in nature

44. **When providing group counseling, a clinician should be _____.**

    A. Able to find a good facility to have the group meet
    B. Knowledgeable about member selection and member and leadership roles in groups
    C. Familiar with systems and strategies of group counseling
    D. Both B and C

45. **In group settings, members often participate in activities that enhance learning and self-exploration. Of the activities listed below, which one is a technique used in Gestalt group therapy?**

    A. Sitting in the hot seat
    B. Creating a mask
    C. Dancing to music
    D. Writing a story

46. **Cognitive Behavioral Group Therapy (CBGT) is particularly effective for which disorder listed below?**

    A. Psychotic Disorder
    B. Schizophrenia
    C. Anxiety Disorder
    D. Borderline Personality Disorder

47. **What type of skills can be taught in a group setting?**

    A. Stress management
    B. Anger management
    C. Social skills training
    D. All of the above

48. **What are two of the aims of group psychotherapy?**

A. To help patients identify maladaptive behaviors and provide a supportive structure for clients
B. To meet new people and learn new social skills
C. To reduce stress and anger
D. None of the above

49. **Are there any concerns about the effects of group psychotherapy?**

A. No concerns. It benefits everyone.
B. Some concerns, but nothing to worry about
C. In some cases, there have been a worsening of symptoms or appearance of new symptoms
D. Lots of concerns; don't try it!

50. **What is a key belief of group therapy?**

A. That the client, as an individual, must initially learn about him or herself before trying to function in a group setting.
B. That although many clients experience emotional pain alone, they can get better when interacting with others facing similar problems.
C. That a client will be more likely to have a more substantial social life if he or she becomes accustomed to being in a group.
D. Both A and C

Human Growth and Development

1. According to Piaget's theory of development, concrete operational thinking occurs between:

    A. Ages 2-6
    B. Ages 12-19
    C. Ages 7-11
    D. Ages 40-49

2. The stage of development titled Identity vs. Role Confusion begins in the teen years according to which theorist?

    A. Freud
    B. Erikson
    C. Maslow
    D. Piaget

3. In Lawrence Kohlberg's moral stages of development, the ability to recognize good and bad intentions in one's self is seen as a:

    A. Social systems perspective
    B. Contractual perspective
    C. Social relationships perspective
    D. Blind egoism

4. The memories children make in middle childhood help to define the consistent and unique pattern of social and emotional behavior and abilities that define an individual. This is called_____.

    A. Personality
    B. Self-Actualization
    C. Human nature
    D. Memorization

5.

Which of the following makes caring for others a focus in development?

    A. Piaget's theory
    B. Psychosocial theory
    C. Psychoanalytic theory
    D. None of the above

6. Adults often experience a gap between their present view of themselves and their memories of childhood. One possible reason for this gap is ____.

    A. The selective way we recall our personal histories
    B. The difficulty we have in seeing ourselves in the same way we view young children
    C. Memory loss
    D. That our past experiences are less important than our present

7. **According to Erikson, during old age, people experience the crisis of _____.**

    A. Trust vs. mistrust
    B. Ego integrity vs. despair
    C. Emotional acceptance vs. rejection
    D. Industry vs. inferiority

8. **Adolescence can be defined as _____.**

    A. A period of most intense growth
    B. A period during which females progress faster than males
    C. A period from the onset of puberty or sexual maturity to adulthood
    D. A period of frustration for parents

9. **According to the parents of Lucy, a 28-month-old, her favorite word is "no." Which of the following theories describes what stage the child has entered?**

    A. Piaget's concrete operational stage
    B. Freud's oral phase of development
    C. Kohlberg's social systems perspective
    D. Erikson's autonomy vs. shame and doubt

10. **The adult spends a great deal of time problem solving. The _____ becomes the most important to the adult thinker.**

    A. Context
    B. Problem
    C. Content
    D. Solution

11. **Common symptoms of bereavement include all of the following except:**

    A. Insomnia and loss of appetite
    B. A strong need for activity
    C. An empty feeling in the stomach
    D. A feeling of tightness in the throat

12. **Jung believed all but which of the following?**

    A. Men and women grow more similar in personality in the second half of adult life
    B. After mid-life, it is possible to reach an optimally mature state
    C. The last half of adult life is more important than the first half
    D. Personality does not change when we age

13. **Mrs. Smith's thinking has improved with age in some areas and declined in others. This description best illustrates which theory of development?**

    A. Psychoanalytic theory
    B. Baltes' selective optimization with compensation
    C. Erikson's age linked tasks
    D. The contextualist lifespan developmental approach

14. **According to McAdams's studies of generativity, _____.**

    A. As we age, our life goals center more around doing for others
    B. As we age, we grow more spiritual
    C. As we age, we become more assertive
    D. As we age, we become more fixed in our ways

15. **All but which of the following are warning signs that an older depressed male is at risk for committing suicide?**

    A. He is socially isolated
    B. He is over 85
    C. He has just retired
    D. He has recently become disabled by a chronic health problem

16. **Our biological maleness or femaleness is called _____, whereas the psychosocial concept of our maleness or femaleness is called _____.**

    A. Gender; sex
    B. Androgyny; chromosomal sex
    C. Sex; gender
    D. Chromosomal sex; androgyny

17. **In some cases, well-meaning people often tell parents to "let the infant cry or you will spoil him/her by picking them up too much." Child development experts state that an infant under six months of age cannot be "spoiled" by responding to their cries and it is essential to respond in a timely manner to ensure appropriate bonding. Which theory and stage of development would support the experts' stance?**

    A. Freud's oral stage of development
    B. Erikson's trust versus mistrust stage of development
    C. Piaget's sensorimotor stage of development
    D. There is no theory supporting this stance

18. **Lev Vygotsky, psychologist, proposed that children learn through interactions with their surrounding culture. This theory is known as the_____ of development.**

    A. Behavioral perspective
    B. Socio-cultural perspective
    C. Psychoanalytic perspective
    D. Intellectual perspective

19. Albert Bandura's basic concepts of his social cognitive theory include all but one of the following. Which selection is not a part of his concepts?

    A. Observational learning
    B. Self-efficacy
    C. Symbolic representation
    D. Reciprocal determinism.

20. A child's ability to include past and future events in their sphere of activity is referred to as _____.

    A. Time revelation
    B. Symbolic representation
    C. Symbolic design
    D. Time conservation

21. Some cultures have unique - or culture-bound - mental disorders. Does this mean a counselor needs to do additional research when he/she is working with a culture other than his/her own?

    A. Absolutely
    B. Only if the case is unusual
    C. Maybe
    D. Not at all; psychological help is universal

22. Does having a male or a female client make a 'cultural' difference?

    A. Yes. Males and females use different descriptions for same-type maladies.
    B. No. They are both simply human beings.
    C. Yes. Males and females are from different planets.
    D. Yes. They have a very different physical, hormonal, and social makeup.

23. Is the concept of 'self' universal or is it a cultural construction?

    A. It is definitely universal
    B. It is a cultural construction
    C. It may vary a little, but it is mostly universal
    D. Only in North America

24. Just as there are unusual cultural-bound disorders, symptoms can be culture specific as well. Which of the following are actual sets of culture-bound symptoms?

    A. Fullness in head, problems with memory, shortness of breath
    B. Ache all over, headaches, upset stomach
    C. Can't sleep, nervous, uptight
    D. All of the above

25. **Schizophrenia is a prime example of a mental disorder that is believed to be culturally universal. There are many cultural-general symptoms, but there are also four major ways schizophrenia differs across cultures. Which one is listed here?**

  A. Delusions
  B. Incoherent speech
  C. Victim of witchcraft
  D. Poor rapport with others

26. **Just as with schizophrenia, depression is also a known disorder to be culturally universal. In addition to the cultural-general symptoms, there are also some cultural-specific symptoms. For instance, in North America guilt is a big cause of depression; but in China, somatization is more frequent than in other parts of the world. However, it is widely accepted that gender is also a big factor in depression. Which gender is more widely affected?**

  A. Men
  B. Women
  C. Very close for both males and females
  D. Neither, as gender has nothing to do with depression

27. **Industrial and Organizational Psychology today involves a lot of business with other cultures. What could be some of the outcomes of ignoring another country's culture?**

  A. Losing important business
  B. Finding yourself in legal trouble
  C. Insulting your clients
  D. All of the above

28. **There are three major methods of reducing cultural clash. Which choice below is not one of them?**

  A. Examine your thought processes
  B. Adjust your behaviors to match the other's culture
  C. Just carry on as you normally would, others will adjust to you
  D. Recognize that culture clashes are emotionally stressful

29. **What is meant by a culturally specific approach to counseling?**

  A. Being fluent in the culture's language
  B. Familiarity with the cultural heritage
  C. Knowledge of a culture's perceptions of society
  D. B and C

30. **Some essential traits of a multicultural counselor are listed below. Which is correct?**

    A. Self-awareness and understanding of one's own cultural history and experiences
    B. Comprehension of one's environmental experiences in mainstream culture
    C. Perceptual sensitivity towards one's personal beliefs and values
    D. All of the above

31. **In understanding a client, a skilled clinician must _____.**

    A. Have sensitivity and understanding of client's values and belief system
    B. Visit the client's country if different from their own
    C. Be from the same culture
    D. None of the above

32. **The process of becoming a culturally skilled clinician is a(n) _____process.**

    A. Interesting
    B. Exciting
    C. Active
    D. Obsolete

33. **When working with a new client whose ethnicity differs from the clinician, what should the clinician ask him/herself?**

    A. Do I understand the client's cultural values and norms?
    B. Do I have stereotypical views of this client's culture that may interfere in the therapeutic process?
    C. Do I speak the client's primary language?
    D. A and B

34. **Culturally skilled clinicians are able to engage in a variety of _____ and _____ helping responses appropriate to the client's ethnicity.**

    A. Interesting and thoughtful
    B. Verbal and nonverbal
    C. Clear and concise
    D. None of the above

35. **In a cultural perspective, what can affect the worldview of a client?**

    A. Religious and/or spiritual beliefs and values
    B. Sports teams
    C. The city in which they live
    D. Mental illness

36. **Self-awareness is crucial to becoming a skilled multicultural counselor. What are two steps to take to increase self-awareness in this area?**

A. Listen to a variety of music and watch others around you
B. Watch a lot of movies and take notes about differences in cultures you see
C. Ask questions about your culture of origin and examine your values
D. Don't worry about self-awareness. It isn't about you.

37. **People from non-western cultures may be uncomfortable with Brief Psychodynamic Therapy for what reason?**

A. BPT takes too long
B. BPT probes into early childhood issues
C. Clinicians are empathetic
D. BPT encourages self-expression

38. **The goal of cognitive therapy is not greater self-awareness, but greater ability to think clearly and cope with life challenges. Would this be a good fit for multicultural counseling?**

A. No, because everyone wants to be more self-aware.
B. Yes, because sharing thoughts is more comfortable than sharing emotions
C. No. Research has shown cognitive therapy to work only in western populations
D. Yes. Cognitive therapy can help everyone.

39. **Gestalt therapy may be uncomfortable for some populations because it tends to be_____.**

A. Free-style
B. Controversial
C. Confrontational
D. Boring

40. **In multicultural counseling, what is a worldview?**

A. The view from the space station
B. A set of beliefs or assumptions that describe reality for that person
C. A perspective or view on the world, conscious and unconscious
D. B and C

41. **How does environment play an important role in human life?**

A. It regulates growth and development.
B. It dictates whether an individual will be hot or cold natured.
C. It dictates the amount of money an individual will make in a lifetime.
D. None of the above.

42. **What constitutes a physical environment?**

   A. Frequent exercising
   B. A tough neighborhood
   C. All physical surroundings
   D. Both A and C

43. **Three main types of environment are physical, _____ , and _____.**

   A. Human and technological
   B. Natural and organic
   C. Developed and undeveloped
   D. Social and psychological

44. **_____ are chemical substances secreted by an endocrine gland or group of endocrine cells that act to control or regulate specific physiological processes.**

   A. Endorphins
   B. Hormones
   C. Steroids
   D. Polypeptides

45. **_____ is the most relevant and basic topic in the science of psychology.**

   A. Self-esteem
   B. Learning
   C. Culture
   D. Social stature

46. **_____ is a major factor in growth and development.**

   A. Athleticism
   B. Social status
   C. Common sense
   D. Reinforcement

47. **Who believed that by observing child development, we may gain knowledge as to how the human species came about?**

   A. Sigmund Freud
   B. Charles Darwin
   C. Erik Erikson
   D. Jean Piaget

48. _____ insisted that children's minds are shaped by certain social and historical context in which they live as well as the children's interaction with adults.

A. Vygotsky
B. Piaget
C. Watson
D. Skinner

49. _____ is a lifelong process of physical, cognitive, and emotional growth and change.

A. Analysis
B. Biology
C. Human development
D. Metamorphosis

50. **A key component of emotional development in a toddler is:**

A. Learning language and communications skills and advancing from single words to complete sentences.
B. Developing an imagination and creating imaginary friends and situations.
C. Developing trust for caregivers who provide for his or her needs.
D. Beginning to imitate the language and behavior of adults.

Helping Relationships

1. **Alfred Adler developed which theory of psychology?**

   A. Psychoanalytic
   B. Analytical
   C. Person-centered
   D. Individual

2. **Adler's Individual Psychology presents a wide range of creative and useful interventions. One of these is listed below. Which is it?**

   A. Avoiding the tar baby
   B. Pushing the envelope
   C. Spitting in the client's soup
   D. Both A and C

3. **In Alfred Adler's Individual Psychology, the phase of treatment known as Exploration and Analysis include which of these areas?**

   A. Promoting insight
   B. Establishing a therapeutic relationship
   C. Lifestyle assessment
   D. Change and reorientation

4. **Karen Horney's view of human nature was positive and optimistic. According to Horney, our potential for growth and self-actualization is present at birth. Even today, many of her concepts have influenced the development of humanistic psychology. She founded which association which still exists today?**

   A. Association for Advancement of Psychoanalysis (AAP)
   B. Association for Advancement of Retired Persons (AARP)
   C. American Psychological Association (APA)
   D. Association for Humanistic Psychology (AHP)

5. **Virginia Satir is often described as the master of _____.**

   A. Short-term therapy
   B. Communication
   C. Choreography
   D. Transference

6. **A basic psychoanalytic defense mechanism is _____.**

   A. Transference
   B. Confrontation
   C. Rationalization
   D. Stick-to-itiveness

7. **In psychoanalytic theory, a defense mechanism is used by the Ego for what purpose?**

    A. To create harmony within the person
    B. To protect people from anxiety
    C. To protect people from attack by thieves
    D. None of the above

8. **The main focus of Bowen's family theory is to bring about change in _____.**

    A. The individual
    B. The family
    C. The couple
    D. Both A and C

9. **Carl Whitaker's approach to family therapy was called _____.**

    A. Symbiotic
    B. Unconscious
    C. Experiential
    D. Structured

10. **One of the primary goals behind Experiential Family Therapy is_____.**

    A. Keeping family secrets
    B. To utilize the best theory to help the family
    C. To reduce defensiveness
    D. Ensure the marriage remains intact

11. **Object Relations theories seek to explain the effects of early experience on development in terms of internalization of experiences with emphasis on objects (other persons). A criticism of this theory is which of the following?**

    A. The lack of emphasis on the role of the father
    B. A view of people as relatively passive victims of parental deficiency
    C. Complex ideas and vocabulary, sometimes compounded by a lack of clarity in definitions
    D. All of the above

12. **Research on Brief Psychodynamic Therapy has shown it to be helpful in treating _____.**

    A. Schizophrenia
    B. Family dysfunction
    C. Depression
    D. None of the above

13. **What treatment goal is not a part of brief psychodynamic therapy?**

   A. Promoting insight
   B. Eliciting feelings
   C. Promoting new learning
   D. In-depth dream interpretation

14. **Person-centered therapy is based on a strong humanistic base. Which of the following characterizes the humanistic view?**

   A. People are capable and autonomous
   B. People are shaped by early parental messages
   C. People have powerful drives
   D. People are difficult and cranky

15. **Person-centered counseling was developed by _____.**

   A. Erik Erikson
   B. Carl Rogers
   C. Karl Marx
   D. Carl Jung

16. **The fundamental goal of existential therapy is _____.**

   A. Helping people find value, meaning, and purpose in their lives
   B. Helping people understand ego defense mechanisms
   C. Helping people facilitate change
   D. Helping people learn how to overcome depression

17. **If I were a Gestalt therapist, I would use which types of therapeutic treatment?**

   A. Spitting in the clients' soup
   B. Role play
   C. Reflection
   D. Visualization

18. **Gestalt therapy has many treatment objectives. Typical goals in therapy might include_____.**

   A. Helping people live in the here and now
   B. Promoting attention, clarity, and awareness
   C. Promoting self-esteem
   D. All of the above

19. **In Narrative therapy, people are seen as _____.**

   A. Relaxed beings who instinctively know how to focus on their concerns
   B. Beings who grow and develop by focusing on the "felt" sense
   C. Interpretive beings who make meaning of their world through the language of their own stories
   D. None of the above

20. **Narrative therapy seems to be especially useful in what type of circumstances?**

    A. When looking for a quick solution to a specific problem
    B. When people are in crisis
    C. When people have been victimized by others
    D. None of the above

21. **In many ways Cognitive therapy is similar to person-centered counseling, Gestalt therapy, and existential therapy. In what way is it different?**

    A. Cognitive therapy focuses on what a person thinks, not feels
    B. Cognitive therapy focuses on dream interpretation
    C. Cognitive therapy focuses on analyzing the actions of the person
    D. Cognitive therapy takes a long time

22. **Aaron Beck is the person who developed which therapy?**

    A. Gestalt therapy
    B. Person-centered therapy
    C. Existential therapy
    D. Cognitive therapy

23. **Cognitive therapists believe a complete case formulation is important in reflecting an in-depth understanding of the client, which allows a clinician to develop a treatment plan that is likely to be successful. What is not an element of a case formulation?**

    A. List of problems and concerns
    B. Hypothesis about the underlying core belief
    C. Understanding of past relationships
    D. Relationship of the core belief to current problems

24. **Labeling the distortion is a part of Cognitive therapy. Which of the following are categories of distorted thinking?**

    A. All-or-nothing thinking
    B. Overgeneralization
    C. Emotional reasoning
    D. All of the above

25. **Albert Ellis developed what type of therapy?**

    A. Rational Emotive Behavior Therapy
    B. Cognitive Therapy
    C. Neuro-linguistic Programming
    D. Cognitive Behavior Therapy

26. **Cognitive therapists believe that the most effective way to help people make positive changes is by _____.**

A. Enabling them to identify, evaluate, and modify their thoughts if needed
B. Enabling them to clarify and interpret emotions
C. Enabling them to keep their thoughts just the way they are
D. Cognitive therapists do not enable people

27. **Research indicates that cognitive therapy is particularly effective in treating what disorder?**

A. Bed wetting
B. Depression and anxiety
C. Schizophrenia
D. Borderline Personality Disorder

28. **Rational Emotive Behavior Therapy (REBT) uses an intervention called disputing irrational beliefs. Which of the following is not one of the four strategies of disputation?**

A. Logical disputes
B. Empirical disputes
C. Didactic disputes
D. Rational alternative beliefs

29. **EMDR is short for _____.**

A. Eye movement desensitization and reprocessing
B. Eight more dead rabbits
C. Eye movement description and reproduction
D. Eye movement desensitization and reunification

30. **A meta-analysis of EMDR (Eye Movement Desensitization and Reprocessing) found that it is very effective for treating which disorder?**

A. Posttraumatic Stress Disorder
B. Depression
C. Substance abuse
D. All of the above

31. **One goal of psychoanalysis is _____.**

A. Changing distorted thought processes
B. Reducing the perfectionism and rigidity of the superego
C. Transferring blame from the superego to the ego
D. Reducing rational thought processes

32. **Jungian Analysis is _____ and _____.**

    A. Light, enriching
    B. Deep, intensive
    C. Short-term, solution focused
    D. Risky, meaningful

33. **Jungian treatment typically has four stages. They are _____.**

    A. Catharsis, elucidation, education, transformation
    B. Interpretation, transformation, summarization, education
    C. Amplification, regression, interpretation, explanation
    D. None of the above

34. **Transactional Analysis (TA) has its roots in which psychological theory?**

    A. Cognitive Behavioral theory
    B. Existential theory
    C. Psychoanalytic theory
    D. Solution-based theory

35. **Who developed Transactional Analysis?**

    A. Aaron Beck
    B. Erik Erikson
    C. The Dali Lama
    D. Eric Berne

36. **J.M. Holden identified four impediments to people's personal and transpersonal development that keep the higher self-underdeveloped or repressed. These blocks to development are:**

    A. Innate (genetic/physiological) factors
    B. Cognitive immaturity
    C. Inexperience limiting knowledge of options
    D. All of the above

37. **Who was B.F. Skinner?**

    A. A cognitive psychologist
    B. A Freudian psychologist
    C. An experimental psychologist
    D. A guitar player for Depeche Mode

38. **Who is well known for his study of the process of using conditioning with dogs?**

    A. John Watson
    B. B.F. Skinner
    C. Isaac Newton
    D. Ivan Pavlov

39. **Albert Bandura played an important role in the development of behavior therapy through his application of principles of both _____ and _____ conditioning to social learning.**

    A. Innate, classical
    B. Classical, operant
    C. Basic, Innate
    D. None of the above

40. **Behavior therapy today is reflected in five models. Which of the following is not one of the five?**

    A. Applied behavioral analysis
    B. Social learning theory
    C. Neo-behaviorism
    D. Cognitive therapy

41. **In Behavioral Therapy, what are two steps in treatment?**

    A. Conceptualize the problem; develop strategies to facilitate change
    B. Review the nature of the problem; analyze clients dreams
    C. Use strategies to change distorted thinking; role play
    D. None of the above

42. **One of the main goals of Behavior therapy is to_____.**

    A. Increase communication skills between couples
    B. Reduce the perfection and rigidity of the superego
    C. Extinguish maladaptive behaviors
    D. Get in touch with the inner child

43. **What therapy was initially developed by William Glasser?**

    A. Gestalt therapy
    B. Reality therapy
    C. Interpersonal therapy
    D. Cognitive behavior therapy

44. **William Glasser believed that people have two basic needs. They are _____ and _____.**

    A. To breathe, to eat
    B. To understand, to love
    C. Relatedness, respect
    D. Worthiness, connectedness

45. **Reality therapists utilize a four step procedure represented as an acronym. It is _____.**

    A. EMDR
    B. NLP
    C. AARP
    D. WDEP

46. **What is Multimodal Therapy?**

   A. Based on the principle of behavior therapy, but systematically integrates strategies from a wide range of approaches.
   B. Developed by B.F. Skinner, it is an approach to therapy based on modeling behaviors
   C. Developed by Arnold Lazarus, its approach pays attention to context
   D. Both A and C

47. **Why might a clinician decide to use an Eclectic approach to counseling?**

   A. No single theoretical model has proven itself superior to the rest
   B. Certain approaches to treatment are more effective than others with particular problems
   C. The growing importance of brief solution-based approaches
   D. All of the above

48. **Existential therapy is not problem or crisis-focused, but involves the establishment of a deep relationship between the _____ and the _____.**

   A. Husband, wife
   B. Client, clinician
   C. Child, parent
   D. Audience, actor

49. **Self-actualization is an important concept for which type of therapy?**

   A. Existential
   B. Psychodynamic
   C. Behavioral
   D. Cognitive

50. **How many levels of cognitions can be categorized in cognitive therapy?**

   A. Two
   B. Three
   C. Five
   D. Four

Research and Program Evaluation

1. What are the three basic elements to look for when assessing a psychology test?

    A. Ease in understanding the questions, length of test, time given
    B. Test style, font used, the phase of the moon
    C. Reliability, validity, standardization
    D. Common element, standardization, biserial correlation

2. What does an 'item characteristic' curve plot?

    A. The responses to each of the options to an item
    B. The item's difficulty against its discrimination
    C. The probability of answering an item correctly against estimates of ability
    D. An individual's responses against the entire group's responses

3. In teacher-made tests, an item analysis is important because:

    A. It reveals correctable features in the test teaching
    B. It informs the teacher as to whether the test should be counted or not
    C. It produces useful technical research data
    D. It supplies students with valuable additional scores

4. What does a self-report personality test examine?

    A. It shows a multiple range of personality traits
    B. It shows one specific personality trait
    C. It shows how multiple personality traits interact
    D. None of the above

5. If you went to a Phrenologist to have your personality tested, how would the expert perform the test?

    A. A paper and pencil test
    B. A projective test (pictures)
    C. An unstructured oral Q & A test
    D. Examine the bumps on your head

6. What is Basic research?

    A. Using the goals of psychology to solve existing real-world problems
    B. Describe, explain, predict, and change behavior
    C. Using the goals of psychology to study behavior simply for knowledge
    D. Research for fun

7. Which of the following is NOT Applied Research?

    A. Research using the principles and discoveries of psychology
    B. Research that's done for practical purposes
    C. Research to solve real-world problems
    D. Research done for study purposes

8. In the realm of psychological research, what procedures belong to research methodology?

    A. Title, Mode of operation
    B. Hypotheses, Variables
    C. Experimentation, Sample
    D. None of the above

9. A Theory is an interrelated set of concepts that is developed in an attempt to explain_____.

    A. The guesses or hunches or beliefs of the one doing the research
    B. The more in depth discussion of experiments
    C. A body of data and to generate testable hypotheses
    D. Whatever it is that the theory wanted explained

10. What is meant by the term "experiment"?

    A. It's a carefully controlled scientific procedure
    B. It's a procedure to see if certain variables have an effect on other variables
    C. It's the gathering of data
    D. Both A and B

11. What is the difference between an independent variable and a dependent variable?

    A. Independent is controlled by experimenter
    B. The dependent is controlled by the experimenter
    C. The dependent is controlled by the participant'
    D. None of these are correct

12. In the world of research, what is meant by a Placebo?

    A. A substance producing no normal physiological effect
    B. Something used as a control technique
    C. Usually used in drug research
    D. All of the above

13. What is the meaning of the 'Placebo Effect'?

    A. When the placebo reacts with someone
    B. When the actual drug being studies does not react with the participant
    C. When the participant reacts as though he took the actual drug, when in fact he received a substance known to produce no effect
    D. When the participant falls asleep due to effects of an ingested chemical

14. **Experimenter bias is the tendency of _____ to influence _____.**

   A. Experimenters, participants
   B. Participants, experimenters
   C. The group, research
   D. Experimenters, the results of the research

15. **In the world of research, a definition of 'sample' is_____.**

   A. A selected group that represents the population
   B. A total of all possible cases in a given area
   C. The drug used in the Placebo Effect
   D. Who cares? At this point, I'm ready for the drug.

16. **A _____ is a tentative explanation for behavior.**

   A. Theory
   B. Hypothesis
   C. Sample
   D. Experiment

17. **Why is an experiment the only way we can determine the cause of a behavior?**

   A. Because of the variables and elimination
   B. Because of one single factor and its effect
   C. Because experiments always work
   D. Because the Placebo Effect uncovers the truth

18. **Which of the following is a non-experimental research technique?**

   A. Correlation
   B. Replicate
   C. Surveys
   D. Perspectives

19. **When researchers systematically record the behavior of participants in their natural state or habitat it is referred to as _____.**

   A. Systematic observation
   B. Informative observation
   C. Scientific observation
   D. Naturalistic observation

20. **What is a case study?**

   A. A study of rare disorders
   B. A study of different cases
   C. An in-depth study of a single subject
   D. All research studies are case studies

21. **Different research designs and strategies are used to gain specific types of information. How does correlational research work?**

A. Investigators assign subjects to groups at random and they receive different levels of a variable.
B. Investigators can't infer causal relationships.
C. Variables are assessed as a function of time.
D. Investigators use naturally occurring groups

22. **When determining test construction, researchers consider the number and type of variables, as well as ethical concerns. When would researchers choose to use multiple-baseline design?**

A. When assignment is not possible
B. When reversal is not possible
C. When selection is not possible
D. When there is not enough data available

23. **In qualitative research like case studies, theory is developed based on data and refines hypotheses. Which of the following statements about case studies is not correct?**

A. They are used to measure attitude, preferences, and satisfaction
B. They are based on the assumption that specific cases can be generalized.
C. They are based on close examination of one case.
D. They are most useful as pilot studies to identify variables to study using different methods.

24. **Meta-analysis is used to study outcomes of therapy and evaluate effectiveness of various therapeutic methods. What does meta-analysis utilize to draw conclusions about outcomes?**

A. Available research literature
B. Feedback from therapists
C. Feedback from patients who have received therapy
D. Effect size of individual studies

25. **There are three types of research design. A study comparing alcohol consumption rates between adolescent males and females is what type of research?**

A. True experimental
B. Quasi-experimental
C. Observational
D. Non-manipulated

26. **There are three main types of group design in research. Which design sometimes requires the process of counterbalancing?**

A. Between groups design
B. Mixed design
C. Passive design
D. Within subjects design

27. **There are three main types of group design in research. Which design involves groups that are both correlated and independent?**

    A. Between groups design
    B. Mixed design
    C. Repeated measure design
    D. Within subjects design

28. **In research, a single-subject design studies one or a few subjects closely, rather than studying groups. What is one of the most common problems associated with single subject design?**

    A. Autocorrelation
    B. Non-manipulation
    C. Carryover effects
    D. Cohort effects

29. **In research, a single-subject design studies one or a few subjects closely, rather than studying groups. Multiple baseline designs resolve common problems associated with other single-subject designs; however they have their own limitations. Which of the following is a problem associated with multiple baseline designs?**

    A. Time investment
    B. Ethical concerns
    C. Threat of history
    D. Failure of variable to return to baseline

30. **Research aims to draw conclusions about relationships among variables. There are a number of threats to validity-factors that interfere with making reliable and clear conclusions. Which of the following concerns is a threat to internal validity?**

    A. Instrumentation
    B. Demand characteristics
    C. Sample characteristics
    D. Experimenter expectancies

31. **Research aims to draw conclusions about relationships among variables. There are a number of threats to validity-factors that interfere with making reliable and clear conclusions. Which of the following is a threat to external validity?**

    A. The Hawthorne effect
    B. The Rosenthal effect
    C. Diffusion
    D. Contact with clients

32.

Which type of research studies the possibility of one variable being the reason another variable happens or changes?

   A. Relational research
   B. Descriptive research
   C. Causal research
   D. None of the above

33.

_____ research attempts to portray what presently exists in a group or population.

   A. Relational
   B. Causal
   C. Rational
   D. Descriptive

34.

_____ research is a study that examines the correlation between two or more variables.

   A. Relational
   B. Descriptive
   C. Causal
   D. Rational

35. **Applied research is a form of research that focuses on _____.**

   A. Solving practical problems
   B. Developing or investigating theoretical questions
   C. Investigating theoretical issues
   D. Finding connections between variables

36. **The _____ is a term that refers to the tendency of some people to work harder and perform better when participating in an experiment.**

   A. Pygmalion effect
   B. John Henry
   C. Hawthorne effect
   D. Placebo effect

37. **The_____ is a set of principles and procedures used by researchers to develop questions, collect data, and come to conclusions.**

    A. Operational method
    B. Scientific method
    C. Hypothesis
    D. Systematic method

38. **_____ research is observational and known as descriptive research as opposed to causal or relational.**

    A. Validity
    B. Longitudinal
    C. Correlational
    D. Cross-sectional

39. **What are some negative factors regarding longitudinal research?**

    A. It cannot establish that one variable causes change in another variable.
    B. It does not allow for scientific control of variables.
    C. Both A and B
    D. None of the above

40. **What is a type of longitudinal research?**

    A. Panel study
    B. Cohort study
    C. Retrospective study
    D. All of the above

41. **What is an advantage of naturalistic observation?**

    A. It may be the only option if a lab is not available
    B. It is quick and affordable, and can be done quickly
    C. Researchers can access data via free databases
    D. Subjects may be aware of being observed and not act as they normally would

42. **The _____ is one of the most common tools used in psychological research.**

    A. Simple experiment
    B. Survey method
    C. Archival research method
    D. Naturalistic observation method

43. **Operant conditioning is also known as**
_____.

    A. Maslow's hierarchy of needs
    B. Self-actualization
    C. Attachment theory
    D. Instrumental conditioning

44. **For what theory is Harvard psychologist Howard Gardener responsible?**

    A. Theory of cognitive development
    B. Psychogenic needs theory
    C. Psychosocial theory
    D. Multiple intelligences theory

45. **A _____ is a subtle hint that lets clients know what the researcher expects to discover or how he or she expects the client to react.**

    A. Demand characteristic
    B. Dependent variable
    C. Descriptive statistic
    D. Selective attrition

46. **Which of the following is one of David Kolb's four learning styles?**

    A. Extroverted style
    B. Judging style
    C. Converger style
    D. All of the above

47. **The primary focus of the Middendorf Breath Experience is;**

    A. To discover the body's own natural response and sensation to the breath as it comes and goes.
    B. To learn how to pass a breathalyzer test.
    C. To learn how to control your breathing while exercising.
    D. None of the above

48. **In classical conditioning, _____ happens when a stimulus is no longer paired with an unconditioned stimulus.**

    A. Acquisition
    B. Discrimination
    C. Extinction
    D. Spontaneous recovery

49. **A _____ is one which neither the researcher nor the participant knows who is receiving a particular treatment.**

    A. Random assignment study
    B. Case study
    C. Single blind study
    D. None of the above

Answers

Human Growth and Development

1.

Answer: C - Intrinsic motivation refers to motivation that comes from within one's own thought or desire. This is the opposite of extrinsic motivation, which is said to come from sources outside one's own thought process.

2.

Answer: B - Extrinsic motivation comes from outside sources, unlike intrinsic motivation, which comes from within the individual. Usually when we think of extrinsic motivation, we think of factors such as money (doing something because it pays you), doing something because you want to prove someone wrong (I'll show you I can do such and such), etc.

Counseling Process

1.

Answers: A and C - Both the lack of transportation and the lack of cultural norms for receiving therapy are both socioeconomic factors that could definitely affect the outcome of therapeutic counseling. If a client does not have transportation to get to and from the counseling session the benefits of counseling would be for naught. If there was a cultural norm that did not approve of therapeutic counseling, the input from family or friends could easily put a stop to the therapy itself or denigrate the outcome.

2. **Answer: B -** Transpersonal and I-You relationships are two of the five types of psychotherapeutic alliances. The other three are: Working alliances, Reparative relationships, and Transferential/countertransferential relationships.

Helping Relationships

1.

Answers: A and B - Transference occurs when a client displaces emotion felt toward a parent or another individual onto the therapist. Countertransference, on the other hand, is an indication of unresolved problems on the part of the helper. The therapist recognizes traits in the client that reminds them of another significant person in their lives and in turn transfers their feelings for that person onto the client.

Professional and Ethical Issues

1.

Answer: B - The duty to warn directive is one instance whereby the therapist might need to break the confidentiality within its code of ethics. If the client is strongly indicating suicide or the harming of someone else, the therapist would probably discuss this with a colleague or supervisor and then act as needed with the decision reached between the therapist and colleague/supervisor. The therapist's duty is to protect his/her client and any person that client might harm.

Human Growth and Development

1.

Answer: A - Social psychologists agree that attitude consists of these three components-the cognitive consisting of thoughts and beliefs, the affective involving feelings, and the behavioral consisting of predispositions to act in certain ways toward an object or situation

2.

Answer: C - The self-serving bias works this way: If we do well on an exam, we tend to think "I really studied" or "I'm pretty smart," but if we do poorly on the exam, we tend to blame the instructor, the textbook, or the "tricky" questions.

3.

Answer: B - As we try to understand our world and the things that go on around us every day, we look for the reasons (or causes) for people's behavior. Clinicians use the term Attribution to describe statements explaining why people do what they do.

4.

Answers: B and C - Age integration can refer to people in any age group and promotes the opportunity for all to work, learn, or play as they wish, regardless of age. Age integration theory draws on a premise of age stratification theory with the idea that society is based on age. This can create age-segregated institutions and acts as a barrier to entrance, exit, or participation. The good news is that we are becoming a more integrated society in many institutions and ways; think of the many universities, colleges, and community learning centers that have young and older students.

5.

Answers: B and C - After age 65, many individuals experience a change in their livelihood Decrease in income, loss of a partner, or deteriorating physical health, are some factors that can contribute to this change; affecting social status. The loss of a long time spouse or partner can cause a wide range of changes and can create a depressed state in most people. Thankfully, there are many individual or group counseling methods involving grief work.

6.

Answers: A and C - It's true - if money is available for better medical care, better and more plentiful food, plus a wider variety of interests and activities, aging will be a healthier and happier process One of the difficulties of measuring the relationship between SES, health, and aging is that occupation is the key status indicator. With the elderly population mostly retired, they are not factored into the data gathered for economic well-being when the data is based on occupation.

Counseling Process

1. **Answer: B** - A comprehensive assessment is used to identify both strengths and problem areas. The seven areas that are assessed are behavior, affect, sensations, imagery, cognitions, interpersonal relationship, and drugs/ biology. This can be represented by the acronym BASIC ID.

2. **Answer: A** - People seem to respond best to interventions that target their preferred modalities. For example, a person who emphasizes imagery is likely to benefit from visualization, while a person who focuses on thinking will probably respond well to identification and modification of cognitive distortions.

3. **Answer: C** - Bridging and tracking are two useful techniques associated with multimodal therapy. In bridging, clinicians deliberately relate to clients first through the client's dominate modality (thinking, feeling, images, etc.) to build connection and rapport, and then branch off into other areas likely to be productive and enhance client skills.

4. **Answer: C** - Imagery is represented by the first "I" in the acronym BASIC ID. Imagery is a modality some may prefer and refers to fantasies, dreams, memories, mental pictures, and one's view of themselves, their lives, and their future.

5. **Answer: B** - People with eating disorders including anorexia nervosa and bulimia nervosa may benefit from Gestalt therapy because they tend to have distorted perceptions of their bodies, dichotomize themselves (separating mind and body), and have problems with contact and boundaries in relationships. Gestalt therapy assists with reconnecting the mind and body and explores distorted perceptions and relationship concerns.

6. **Answer: C** - In this treatment approach, questions usually begin with "what" or "How" or sometimes "where," but rarely with "why." Questions such as "What are you experiencing when you fight with your spouse" or "How does it feel when you fight with your spouse?" are more likely to keep the client in the present moment. 'Why' questions typically lead to a focus on past experiences.

7. **Answer: B** - Goals and therapeutic alliance are a vital part of person-centered counseling. In this type of counseling, it is more a way of being with clients and giving them conditions that will facilitate change, than it is developing a specific treatment plan filled with interventions.

8. **Answer: B -** In person-centered therapy, a clinician creates an environment that allows people to trust themselves and make good use of their potential. They do not interpret dreams or create behavioral interventions for the client. A counselor's acceptance and understanding of their clients, respect for the clients' experiences, and active participation in the treatment process empowers clients to make change.

Helping Relationships

1.

Answers: B and C - Clinician self-disclosure may be used judiciously when it enhances the collaborative nature of the client-clinician relationship or when providing a different perspective. Clinician self-disclosure may also be used to provide useful feedback and to normalize a client's reactions.

Counseling Process

1. **Answer: A -** The fundamental goal in existential therapy is helping people find value, meaning, and purpose in their lives. Existential therapy is a process in which two people go on a journey to assist the client cope more effectively with the conditions of life and make better use of their potential.

2. **Answer: C -** Disputing and replacing cognitions are steps taken in cognitive therapy after the distorted cognitions have been identified, discussed, and categorized. In this disputing and replacing process, the client and clinician work together to find alternative cognitions that have more validity and are more likely to be helpful to the client.

Human Growth and Development

1.

Answer: D - Jumping to conclusions is a type of distorted thinking that can occur when a person takes an action or lack of an action and immediately assumes something else has happened; "Don and I had a fight this morning and now he is late coming home from work. I think he has left me." All or nothing thinking, overgeneralization, and mental filtering are also types of distorted thinking.

Counseling Process

1. **Answer: A** - Sessions are carefully planned and structured to maximize the impact and efficiency of cognitive therapy. People complete inventories and intake questionnaires before beginning treatment. Clinicians review these in order to be well prepared. Each session has an agenda and clear goals to work toward.

2. **Answer: C** - Leading the client in a series of free associations is a therapeutic tool for psychoanalysis, not cognitive therapy. The remaining seven procedures Beck recommends are as follows: determine and measure the intensity of the person's mood, educate the person about cognitive therapy and the role of the client, provide information about the person's difficulties and diagnosis, recommend tasks and homework between sessions, summarize the session, and obtain the client's feedback on the sessions.

3. **Answer: B** - A case formulation allows clinicians to develop a treatment plan that is likely to be successful. It includes six elements including a list of problems and concerns, hypotheses about the core belief or schema, relationship of this believe to current problems, precipitants of current problems, understanding of the background relevant to the core belief, and anticipated obstacles to treatment.

4. **Answer: B** - The first step in changing a behavior is describing that behavior in terms that are specific and measurable according to behavioral therapists. If appropriate, both the undesirable behavior and the desirable change should be specified. Helping people make behavior change involve a series of relatively structured and predictable steps.

5. **Answer: D** - The client and clinician need to agree on how to measure the behavior and ways to record the measurement. Two of the most common methods of measuring behavior are frequency and severity. Generally, people in treatment are encouraged to keep a record of their own behaviors by using a checklist, diary, or other written record of the frequency and severity of the undesirable behavior.

Assessment and Diagnosis

1. **Answer: A** - The term crisis can be applied to a single or recurring problem that is overwhelming or traumatic to an individual. It may be a reaction to being involved in a natural disaster such as a tornado or a hurricane. It can be related to a personal assault, an accident, or war.

2. **Answer: D** - Crisis counseling usually lasts one to three months, or until the client is stabilized and can resume normal functioning. Normal functioning includes tasks such as returning to work, taking care of oneself and others, and meeting his/her needs on a daily basis.

3. **Answer: D** - In a crisis situation, a counselor may work with law enforcement agencies, FEMA, and state Health and Human Services, as well as other private organizations such as domestic violence shelters, the Red Cross, United Way, and local community organizations.

4. **Answer: B** - Children and elderly people require special care after a natural disaster. Children experience the same reactions as adults, but they lack the experience, vocabulary, and conceptual ability necessary to deal with such situations. In the case of the elderly, natural disasters can increase the feeling of loss, resulting in further social isolation, and can increase feelings of depression and inability to effect positive change in their lives.

5. **Answer: D** - Some of the reasons to provide outreach within a community are to reach an underserved population, to increase public awareness, and to link resources with other agencies with similar purposes. Another reason may be to focus on an event or issue that is underrepresented in an area.

6. **Answer: D** - A mental health clinic can provide psycho educational classes at the senior center, mental health information sent via traditional mail services, and brief solution-focused therapy. After determining the type of outreach needed, those involved need to find a funding source for the proposed outreach and to identify staffing resources and location.

7. **Answer: D** - Grants, revenue from services, and fund raising events are all examples of funding resources for mental health outreach programs. Private foundations are often looking for programs enhancing community services and match their ideology. State, local, and Federal governments also have grant money to disburse to community programs. Profit from other mental health services as well as fund-raising events might also contribute to resources for community outreach.

8. **Answer: A** - To manage a counseling program effectively, a person must have supervisory and administrative skills. Having knowledge of a variety of approaches to supervision may be necessary in managing a group of professional and paraprofessional workers. Administrative skills such as time management, ability to coordinate services, effective communication skills and the ability to collaborate with other agencies are necessary as well if management is to be effective.

9. **Answer: B** - Program management involves integrating teaching and counseling skills. Training is an integral component of an organization and the skilled manager needs to be comfortable in a teaching role and able to conduct in-service training programs in a variety of areas. The manager may or may not facilitate and plan events for the organization.

10. **Answer: C** - Program managers can build rapport by sponsoring community events and inviting other agencies to collaborate in planning and execution, or by joining committees focused on relevant community goals. They can also initiate collaboration by inviting other community agencies to plan and execute a community event sponsored by the home agency. In short, being visible in the community requires both time and commitment to develop the relationships needed to produce positive change.

11. **Answer: D** - As a member of a multi-disciplinary team, you might be expected to chair a committee, organize an event, and attend weekly meetings. For example, you may be asked to chair a committee researching the best method to bring services to an underdeveloped area of the community. Or you may be asked to organizing public awareness events and/or attend weekly meetings to meet the goals of the team.

12. **Answer: A** - A multi-disciplinary team is a group of professionals from a variety of fields (or disciplines) that have joined together for a particular purpose. A task force for reducing domestic violence might include counselors, law enforcement personnel, domestic violence shelter staff, state health and welfare workers, as well as other members of the community interested and involved in this concern.

13. **Answer: C** - Traffic violations do not fall under the realm of mental health services and would not be a focus of a multidisciplinary team involving a counselor. Domestic violence, substance use, teen pregnancy, rural health care, child abuse and neglect are all examples of likely teams a mental health worker might be asked to participate in on behalf of their agency.

14. **Answer: C** - With a state prison in the area, there may be a population of partners and children of the inmates living within the local community in need of mental health services. These needs may be addressed through support groups, school systems, and public awareness campaigns increasing awareness of services. A multidisciplinary team may be established to determine the needs of this population and generate ideas for services.

15. **Answer: C** - Research has shown that cognitive behavior therapy is effective in smoking cessation programs. Additionally, evidence indicates that this type of therapy is useful for treating mental health disorders such as eating disorders, depression, anxiety, and obsessive-compulsive disorders. Treatment is well planned and structured, focusing on changing thoughts and behaviors.

16. **Answer: D** - Support groups can be an effective form of treatment for a variety of issues, including divorce, parenting a child with disabilities, and grief. Through this venue, participants receive strength and encouragement from group members, allowing them to work out the issues involved and to learn vicariously through the experiences of others. With a skilled facilitator, group work can be particularly helpful as it allows the members to try out behaviors and new skills in a controlled, unthreatening environment.

17. **Answer: D** - Persons with autism spectrum disorders may not be good candidates for group work. Persons involved in group work need to have clear mental abilities, be able to focus on the here and now, and be capable of interacting socially, providing support and feedback when needed. People with autism spectrum disorders are more inwardly focused, have difficulty interacting with others, and may not have the communication skills necessary to participate in a group format.

18. **Answer: A** - REBT has been shown to be effective in treating mild to moderately severe mental health disorders such as depressive disorders, anxiety disorders, and adjustment disorders. It may also help some of the milder personality disorders (e.g. avoidant and dependent personality disorders) make important and pervasive changes. It is not recommended for treating traumatic childhood concerns due to its direct, somewhat confrontational stance. People with psychotic disorders may not have the ability to focus on cognitive distortions and thus would not find REBT to be helpful in treatment.

19. **Answer: C** - Solution-based brief therapy is particularly well suited to treatment of anxiety and depression, as well as problems of adjustment. As with other cognitive and behavioral approaches, it does not work well with people who pose a danger to themselves and others, or those who are suffering from psychosis or dissociative identity disorders.

20. **Answer: D** - Treatment goals for brief solution-based therapy need to be meaningful and important to clients, need to be small and within easy reach rather than large and challenging, and need to be written down, with a copy for both the client and clinician. Additionally, goals should be realistic and achievable, measurable and within the client's control.

21. **Answer: D** - The "D" in BASIC ID stands for drugs/biology. This is broadly defined as biological functioning, including overall health, nutrition, exercise, and self-care. It encompasses any type of substance use or misuse as well. The other letters in the acronym stand for Behavior Affect, Sensations, Imagery, Cognition, and Interpersonal factors.

22. **Answer: C** - One of the goals of Developmental Counseling and Therapy (DCT) is to help people gain more integration, organization, flexibility, and range in their cognitive development structures. The DCT clinician promotes growth and change through exploration and assessment of people's world views, operations in the world, and areas of difficulty and cognitive developmental orientations.

23. **Answer: A** - In DCT, the sensorimotor environmental structuring is a process that provides direction, promotes awareness and direct experience, focuses attention on the here and now, and minimizes denial and splitting. Some of the interventions that clinicians use in this stage are the Gestalt empty chair technique, body work such as yoga and massage, relaxation, guided imagery, and environmental change.

24. **Answer: D** - A clinician can gain self-knowledge through inventories such as the MBTI and through listening to feedback received from others. This knowledge, combined with information on the treatment systems, can help a clinician find their clinical approach by mating the theoretical approach that seems best suited to them at any point in their career.

25. **Answer: C** - Most of the questions on the MMPI test are about abnormal behavior because it is designed for clinical and counseling psychologists to diagnose psychological disorders. It is grouped into ten clinical scales, each measuring a different disorder.

26. **Answer: B** - The difference between the MMPI-1 and the MMPI-2 is that the MMPI-2 is a revision of the MMPI-1. The MMPI-1 was developed during the 1930's and contains many cultural and racial biases. A revision was completed in 1989 to correct these biases, including gender references and outmoded idiomatic expressions. The result is the MMPI-2.

27. **Answer: D** - All of the options listed in this question describe the Rorschach test. The Rorschach Inkblot test is a projective test created by a Swiss psychiatrist (Hermann Rorschach) in the 1900's that involves showing subjects cards of abstract inkblots and having them interpret concrete images from them. The idea behind the test is that the differences in perception relate to differences in personalities.

28. **Answer: A** - A test using cards that portray human figures in a variety of settings and situations in called the Thematic Apperception Test. The Thematic Apperception Test is a projective test created by Henry Murray in 1938. It is mainly used by psychoanalytically trained therapists. The underlying theory is that the test's respondents identify with the main character and project their psychological needs and conflicts into the story they tell using the cards.

29. **Answer: C** - Two of the criticisms of projective tests are that interpreting the results of the tests depends too much on the subjective judgment of the examiner, and that the reliability and validity of projective tests is the lowest of all the personality tests.

30. **Answer: B** - Systematic observation is the process of observing behavior as it is occurring. Systematic observation begins with casually observing a subject then using a systematic means to collect data. Some refer to this as "people watching."

31. **Answer: C** - Another way an expectancy table can be used in counseling is to provide clients with information on how they might succeed in a particular area. For example, when deciding upon a career path, one might use an expectancy table to calculate the likelihood of success in any given career. The higher the score indicated on the table, the more likely you are to succeed at a career.

32. **Answer: B** - When a client first starts counseling, it is imperative to have supportive surroundings. Although some clients may feel the need to post their issues on Facebook and reliable transportation is also important, counseling will not succeed unless the client surrounds him or herself with a supportive infrastructure. A supportive infrastructure might include friends and family or a club whose activities are not detrimental to the client's counseling. For example, one who is seeking counseling for alcohol issues would probably not want to be around people or groups who frequent bars.

33. **Answer: C** - A main aspect of test development using the empirical approach is the construction of comparison groups. A group of close friends and family to support the client is important, but not a main aspect of test development. Having the capability to maneuver through the obstacles one encounters in one's own life and the world and how one interacts in the world is the existential approach.

34. **Answer: A** - A preliminary step in utilizing tests in counseling is letting the expectations of the test be known. It is important for both the counselor and the client to know what the expected outcome is and how they are going to go about attaining that outcome. This step may take more than one session as this can lead to negotiations until realistic expectations are agreed upon.

35. **Answer: A** - Testing should not be the sole source of collecting data about a client because assembling information from a variety of means helps to create a broader comprehension of the client and his or her issues. Other means of gathering information can include interviews or observation. A multi-faceted information collection strategy that includes all of these methods will most effectively indicate what is really going on with the client.

36. **Answer: C** - No, assessment is an ongoing process throughout counseling and does not stop once the counseling begins. A client may develop new symptoms during counseling, which may or may not be detected without further assessment beyond the initial testing. A counselor can then alter the treatment plan for the client to address the new issues.

37. **Answer: B** - Another reason to continue testing throughout the term of counseling is that ongoing assessment will bring to light new needs that may have surfaced during counseling. These needs can then be addressed in conjunction with the initial problems. Continuous assessment lets both the counselor and client know what a client's needs are throughout the counseling process.

38. **Answer: D** - Role playing plays a part in qualitative assessment by providing the counselor with insight as to how the client behaves in a given situation and providing the client with an alternative way to handle a situation. During role play the counselor can discuss why the client is reacting the way he or she is to the situation. The client can then see what the outcome might have been had an alternate reaction been chosen.

39. **Answer: B** - In the counseling assessment process, the counselor is responsible for obtaining or bringing forth information needed for successful counseling. The counselor should not rely solely on information provided by the client or family members as this information may be one-sided and may not provide the complete picture. The counselor should use a variety of means to bring as much information to the surface as possible.

40. **Answer: A** - Integral therapy involves assessing the many intertwined parts of a client, including biological, cognitive, emotional, rational, and spiritual. This approach brings to light a more thorough comprehension of the client and his or her surroundings. The counselor can then decide upon a counseling plan.

41. **Answer: D -** Cognitive therapy was developed by Aaron T. Beck. Cognitive therapy focuses on changing a client's attitudes, perceptions, and thinking. It may include interventions meant to help a client see and correct inappropriate thoughts and beliefs.

42. **Answer: B** - Yes, the difference between regression therapy and psychodynamic therapy is regression therapy is more solution-focused and psychodynamic therapy is more about the process and the experience of coming to a solution. Regression therapy focuses on finding a solution to a problem by helping the client to revisit his or her past to find trouble spots, then working to understand feelings and thoughts. Psychodynamic therapy first treats the client's present-day issues and then works to acknowledge the existence of a pre-existing problem from the past, working to develop goals for change.

43. **Answer: B** - Free association and building a strong therapeutic alliance are some techniques used in psychodynamic therapy. Other techniques include recognizing resistance and transference, working through painful memories and difficult issues, and catharsis. A main belief in psychodynamic therapy is that problems develop mainly from early childhood events.

44. **Answer: C -** One of the goals of clients who engage in existential therapy is to face their fears and overcome them through action. By overcoming these fears, the client is able to dictate the course he or she wants to take. This gives the client a sense of freedom from letting his or her fears dictate their actions.

45. **Answer: D** - Motivational Enhancement Therapy is mainly used to treat addictions. Clients facing alcohol and drug abuse, among other addictions, can benefit from undergoing this type of therapy. Motivational Enhancement Therapy is especially beneficial to juveniles facing addictions.

46. **Answer: A** - A type of therapy that centers on the belief that knowledge is the result of social rhetoric and conversation is collaborative therapy. Furthermore, this type of therapy asserts that a person's actions are based upon the comprehension of this knowledge. The goal of collaborative therapy is to unify knowledge in such a way that will provide an answer to a client's problems.

47. **Answer: C** - Schema therapy is used to treat eating disorders. Depression and other personality issues can also be treated using Schema therapy. Schema therapy takes place in a compassionate and understanding setting so that the client feels comfortable discussing his or her past. Problems can then be identified and dealt with accordingly.

48. **Answer: B** - The main aspect of family therapy is that a person must reflect on childhood memories he or she has and learn from them how to flourish in relationships. This reflection plays a leading part in how we navigate all other relationships. If we have a more insightful understanding of ourselves as we interact amid our family system, we can become more adaptable in all of our relationships.

Career Development

1. **Answer: B** - The definition of I/O reads: The study of how individual behavior affects and is affected by the physical environment and the organizational structure of the workplace.

2. **Answer: D** - There are three primary areas of interest for I/O psychologists. They are human factors, personnel, and organizational psychology.

3. **Answer: D** - Human Factor Psychology addresses each of the factors listed in this question. It seeks to improve the design and function of machines and the work environment to better meet the needs of human users. For example, Human factors psychologists help design controls and displays in automobiles. They also helped design the ATM machines.

4. **Answer: C** - The Personnel branch of I/O psychology involves the recruiting, selecting, training, and evaluating of workers. It plays an important role in locating the right person for the right job.

5. **Answer: A** - An employee performance evaluation tells a company any concerns that an employee may have and identifies training needs and present employee skill level. One on one time with a supervisor can be a bonding feature for all types of concerns, job situations, praise, and future training needs.

6. **Answer: B** - A job analysis is a detailed description of the tasks involved in a job, the relationship between that job and other jobs, and the knowledge, skills, and abilities necessary to perform the job successfully.

7. **Answer: D** - All of the choices listed in this question are true statements about sexual harassment. Unfortunately, sexual harassment is still very much a part of many work environments. One of the misconceptions about it is that it is often reported. A survey has found that of the women that were harassed, 75% ignored the harassment and only 18% reported the harassment. It's not reported often for all of the above reasons. Although it appears to be less common in men, they can also be victims of sexual harassment.

8. **Answer: D** - Sexual harassment is primarily an assertion and abuse of power. People often mistakenly believe that sexual harassment is primarily an expression of sexual desire.

9. **Answer: D** - The two basic types of managers are those (theory X) that are negative towards their employees and always looking for the wrong, and those (theory Y) that take a positive outlook with their employees and look for (and find) the best in each one.

10. **Answer: A** - Participative Decision Making is a decision making model in which the people involved in implementing a decision are also involved in making it. This strategy promotes team work and avoids conflicts between managers and employees.

11. **Answer: B** - The three theories are Equity Theory, Goal-Setting Theory, and Expectancy Theory. Equity theory says that we are strongly motivated to maintain a state of equilibrium or balance. In a work setting, employees prefer jobs in which the output is equal to the input. If imbalances occur, workers adjust their input, output, or their psychological perceptions.

12.

Answer: C - Job satisfaction results from a match between personality and occupation according to the Trait and Factor Theory of Occupational Choice. Supportive colleagues, supportive working conditions, mentally challenging work, and equitable rewards are also important.

13. **Answer: C** - A lack of knowledge about how to interview is not associated with "First date" syndrome. In initial interview meetings with important, but unstated outcomes, both parties behave with artificial care and skill.

14. **Answer: A** - Interviewees are tense and anxious because they are being evaluated and compared to others and because they need what the employer has to give.

15. **Answer: B** - First impressions are often characterized as subjective. When one person meets another for the first time, sometimes nothing more than clothes or facial appearance helps to form a first impression.

16. **Answer: D** - Taking charge of the interview is not generally an effective strategy for interviewees. It helps with interviewing if, prior to the interview, you research the job and company so you can better formulate your answers. It is also helpful to role play your interview with a friend or family member. It helps to remember that being your own friendly, eager, and assertive self has helped you in previous first meetings of any kind.

17. **Answer: C** - The halo effect is the tendency to rate individuals either too high or too low on the basis of one outstanding trait. The halo effect is a characteristic defect in rating scales. An example would be judging a good looking person as more intelligent.

18. **Answer: A** - The major unstated goal of orientation is to transmit organizational culture. Within each organization, a distinct culture exists, complete with taboos, traditions, assumptions, etc. It is helpful for a new employee to look beyond what is being said and "read between the lines" to get some insight into company culture.

19. **Answer: B** - Helping people develop skills like resume writing and interviewing techniques are some of the things career counselors do to create a more effective job search. Other skills they might teach include post-interview etiquette, the 30-second "sound bite" of personal information, and dressing for success.

20. **Answer: D** - When meeting with a client, a career counselor might utilize all of the options listed in this question. Career counseling involves using a wide variety of inventories designed to assess interests, abilities, and values to help the client pinpoint career goals. The counselor may also assist the client in self-exploration and values clarification to further the likelihood for setting goals that will be successful. They may also teach a variety of skills such as decision-making, effective goal setting, and life planning.

21. **Answer: B** - According to social cognitive career theory, many people eliminate occupational choices because they have faulty self-efficacy beliefs or low expectations of their ability to perform in certain types of jobs. People with low confidence in math or science may eliminate any engineering or medical careers because of their belief they would not be able to perform well academically.

22. **Answer: C** - In social cognitive career theory, counselors may assist their clients in analyzing their perceptions of barriers to a career and identifying closed occupational possibilities. Some clients may believe there are too many barriers (e.g. lack of math skills) to certain types of careers. Counselors may work with clients to change those perceptions and problem solve with their clients to remove those possible barriers. There may also be misperceptions held regarding the career types and counselors can help clients identify previously closed occupational possibilities, such as engineering for women or nursing for men.

23. **Answer: B** - A social cognitive career counselor may assist their client in modifying a faulty self-efficacy belief by helping them develop new performance beliefs and reanalyze past experiences that have led to the faulty beliefs they hold. An example may be a person who believes they cannot learn to use a computer based on a past experience. A counselor may enroll them in a basic computer class and as the person learns computer skills, they also develop new performance beliefs about the computer and can then reanalyze the faulty belief that they could not have a career that had anything to do with computers.

24. **Answer: B** - The Occupational Outlook Handbook, or OOH, is a valuable source of information about careers. Such informational can include the outlook or forecast of the career, potential salary, where jobs of this type might be found, education requirements, etc. Many career counselors consider it to be the foremost resource for researching careers.

25.

Answer: C - Donald Super is the creator of the Archway Model of Career Determinants theory. His theory has five stages: growth, exploration, establishment, maintenance, and decline. Each stage is based along a time line but varies in the exact age that each stage is reached. His theory emphasizes self-concept and vocational adjustment through the lifespan.

26. **Answer: C** - There are six vocational types in Holland's career theory. These are based on a behavioral style or personality approach to career choices and include Realistic, Investigative, Artistic, Social, Enterprising, and Conventional. Individuals choose multiple choice answers on a test, which are components of the six areas. The scores from this test give the person an indication of where his or her interests lie regarding vocational types.

27. **Answer: A** - Self-efficacy is an individual's belief in their ability to organize and perform the actions required to produce a desired outcome. In Bandura's theory, self-efficacy is based on personal performance, vicarious experiences, verbal persuasion, and physiological and emotional factors. Self-efficacy plays a central role in motivation. The person who believes they can do something, will try and keep trying until they have accomplished what they intended.

28. **Answer: C** - A person who scores highly in the Realistic area of Holland's vocational types is someone who likes to work with their hands, machines, and tools. They like to be actively working, not sitting at a desk, and are often seen in jobs that involve working outdoors such as construction, farming, and letter carrier.

29. **Answer: D** - Life roles describe how we take on a variety of roles in life as we age and how we view ourselves. In career counseling, one's life roles are taken into consideration throughout the career path. In one stage of life, a person might be seen as a 'student' and the focus is on education. Or they might be seen as 'breadwinner' and the focus is on earning a wage to support a family. Future roles may need to be examined in career counseling to ensure a good fit. At a later stage, one's role might be 'physician' as well as 'mother.' How well these fit together may be because of a preemptive look at the possibility of taking on both roles prior to entering into training to become a physician, especially if the woman values the role of 'mother' for later in life.

30. **Answer: B** - In the mid-teens and early twenties, the major theme is exploration. In this stage, the major task is to develop a healthy self-concept and examine the possibilities of career through role tryouts and exploration, eventually leading to narrowing the choices of career and pursuing that choice. Some people may rapidly advance through this stage while others may linger.

31. **Answer: A** - A time frame for reaching your career goals should be included in your career goal plan. Your career goals may also include a job you want to be eligible for in the future. You should keep in mind your goals should be realistic and attainable.

32. **Answer: C** - Studies that have examined counselors' skills have found that the most under-skilled counselors tend to be the most likely to overestimate their performances. It has been found that the skills needed to perform well are also the skills needed to assess one's own performance. If this is the case, a counselor may not only be poorly skilled, but also lack the tools needed to discover his or her weaknesses.

33. **Answer: A** - Employment options for counselors include starting your own practice, joining an established practice, and working in an academic setting. Working in an academic setting allows a new counselor the opportunity to begin a new career while remaining in a familiar setting. It allows the counselor to work without the stress of dealing with new surroundings.

34. Answer: D - Some of the negative factors counselors may face when beginning their careers include incompetence, licensing and credentialing, and ethical and legal concerns. Another negative factor is that there may be a major reliance upon outside expertise to practice therapy. Beginning a new career can be an enormous strain on new counselors, and they will need to be prepared to deal with issues as they arise.

35. Answer: C - Some personal concerns a new counselor may face are the need for recognition and balancing personal and professional life. Another personal concern is financial strain. It is helpful for a new counselor to seek out an experienced colleague for guidance.

36. Answer: D - One question a counselor must consider when deciding how to continue his or her career path is, "Is this the right environment for me"? Other questions may include, "Are my needs being fulfilled through my counseling work"? and "How does my counseling career fit in with my long-term goals"? A significant amount of thought should occur when deciding upon continuing a career path as a counselor.

37. Answer: B - A common problem veteran counselors may have if they remain in an academic setting is that they may not be able to relate to their students due to the age difference. As a counselor gets older, new younger counselors enter the workforce. This can either be a hindrance or an opportunity for the veteran counselor to become a mentor.

38. Answer: B - If a counselor cannot find professional support and helpful resources, a lack of commitment may result. Additionally, the counselor may be less willing to invest significant effort in his or her work. This may happen at any stage of a counselor's career, although reasons and results may vary.

39. Answer: D - The development of a career ladder listing attainable promotions within the company can make a counselor want to remain in the same job for an extended period. If a counselor has a goal, such as a promotion, he or she is likely to remain with the same company. Tenure is also a possible benefit for remaining with the same company.

40. **Answer: B** - Promoting involvement at the local, regional, and national levels will help foster professional development within a company. As a counselor, you can become involved in events and organizations on any level you aspire to. This will lead to more experience and exposure for you, thus helping you further your career.

41. **Answer: D** - Supporting flexible schedules will help a company maintain a low turnover rate among counselors by allowing counselors the freedom to attend to the needs of their families. It will also give counselors the ability to run essential errands and appointments without using personal time. Offering a flexible schedule is a major benefit an employer can offer.

42. **Answer: A** - It is advisable to have a plan in mind for the next five or ten years so you will always have a goal toward which to work. If you have goals, you will have a way to measure the progress of your career. If you have no goals, it may seem like you are working for no reason.

43. **Answer: D** - In-house or external training, conferences and workshops, and work-based research are all ways you can further your professional career. Other ways include attending seminars and reading professional magazines and journals. Make sure you keep any receipts or certificates you receive.

44. **Answer: B -** Keeping up with technology can help you further your career. Society keeps manufacturing faster and easier ways to do things. Force yourself to keep up with the latest advances in technology.

45. **Answer: B** - Building and maintaining a professional network will be invaluable as the role of the counselor changes. This network will be extremely important as your career evolves. It can help you in your current position or provide opportunities if you have doubts about where you are headed in your career.

46. **Answer: C** - A good counselor will take notice of changes and trends in the economy and in his or her profession. The future cannot be accurately predicted. Stay ahead of the game by keeping yourself informed on what is going on around you.

47. **Answer: C** - It is important for you to build a reputation consistent with your career goals. Remember that actions speak louder than words. Reputation can take years to build but can be destroyed in seconds.

48. **Answer: B** - Henry Ford said, "You can't build a reputation on what you say you are going to do." What you do means a great deal more than what you say about yourself or your achievements. How you are viewed by your peers and your clients can make or break your career.

49. **Answer: B** - Good learning and information skills are imperative for successful counselors. When beginning your career you must study a large quantity of information so that you will be an effective counselor. As your career develops, it will be increasingly necessary to continue to process updated information.

Professional and Ethical Issues

1. **Answer: A** - One reason to declare incompetency in a practice is working with a client in an area where education or training has not been completed. Knowing a client's ethnicity is greatly recommended and working with a physical disability should not be a problem to a counselor.

2. **Answer: D** - After thoroughly informing the client of all aspects of the counseling, such as fees, style, and expectations of both parties, the counselor then asks for either a written or oral (or both) consent.

3. **Answer: B** - Dual relationships usually cause a counselor to lose objectivity and effectiveness, therefore they are considered unethical. There is occasionally a relationship between client and counselor that is considered ethical if it can reasonably be expected to cause no harm to, or exploitation of, the client.

4. **Answer: D** -None of the options listed are people with whom counseling practitioners may fully discuss clients. Practitioners discuss confidential matters of their work only for appropriate scientific or professional reasons and only with other professionals that are concerned with such matters.

5. **Answer: D** - All of the above factors are directly related to the research process. Plagiarism, or using someone else's work, is absolutely unethical. Great care is taken to see that any animals used in research are given the most comfortable and humane treatment possible. The institutional approval is often required, and correct and factual note taking is a must. Fabrication of material is a definite no-no.

6. **Answer: C** -In a clinical test, the client has the right to receive pertinent information before giving consent to participate. Furthermore, the client has the right to approve or deny in writing the publication of results of the test. The client also has the right to an interpreter if necessary. Of course, there may be extenuating circumstances that need special care.

7. **Answer: D** - All counseling ethics do apply, along with some specific ones to deal with the special circumstances involved with school counseling. Furthermore, school counselors have an association (ASCA) and the association has a book (School Counseling Principle: Ethics and Law) that specializes in helping the counselor deal with the difficult and unusual (and sometimes emergency) situations. School counselors are in the midst of a wide variety of counseling situations every day spent at the schools. They are dealing with 'minors' with all ranges of problems, including suicides.

8. **Answer: D** - Parents sometimes get caught up in the issues between husband and wife and forget to remain focused on what is best for the children. Of course there is a tremendous amount of stress for everyone during this major life change, however often times the children's stress gets pushed to the background.

9. **Answer: D** - The preamble to the above publication of 1990 instructs psychologists to maintain their competence, retain objectivity in applying their skills, and preserve the dignity and best interests of their clients, colleagues, students, research participants, and society.

10. **Answer: C** - Gestalt psychology was founded by German psychologists and focuses on principles of perception and the organized whole. Psychobiology roots began from the beginnings of experimental physiology and a belief that problems had a biological cause. Humanistic psychology emphasizes the uniqueness of the individual. These schools and their founders have contributed greatly to the development of psychology as we know it today.

11. **Answer: D** - Structuralism focused on the sensations and feelings of conscious experience and established the importance of studying mental processes.

12. **Answer: A** -The history of psychology and all its many forms have significantly affected the psychology methods or practices we use today. Our modern psychologists talk about basic perspectives that influence the topics that are taught today. These include, but are not limited to, the psychoanalytic, behavioristic, humanistic, cognitive, and biological perspectives. We refer to it as an Eclectic view.

13. **Answer: D** - Freud's theory is still controversial and receives a lot of criticism today for all of the reasons listed in this question. Freud's concept of the conscious, unconscious, and preconscious mind was a new and intriguing idea. Couple that with his techniques for uncovering hidden, unconscious motives - and you have cause for much controversy and criticism. Add the fact that his work was based on individual case studies, all of which involved people with 'abnormal' thoughts and behaviors without comparison to 'normal' people's thoughts and behaviors. Although his theories are still controversial and still receive much criticism, Freud had a major impact on psychotherapy and psychiatry development and he can be credited with much of the growth of psychology throughout the world.

14. **Answer: B** - Some of the degrees available in psychology are DMFT, PhD, and PsyD. The DMFT stands for Doctor of Marriage and Family Therapy, PhD is Doctor of Philosophy, and PsyD is Doctor of Psychology. MA and MS stand for Master's Degree in specific areas and LPsy is the EU and Latin America's degree designation equivalent for the American PsyD.

15. **Answer: D** - Professional licenses for the Master degrees include LMFT, CRC, LPC, LCSW, LPC, LMHC. The LMFT is Licensed Marriage and Family Therapist; CRC stands for Certified Rehabilitation Counselor; LPC is Licensed Professional Counselor (some states), or LMHC (some states) for Licensed Mental Health Counselor; and LCSW is Licensed Clinical Social Worker.

16. **Answer: B** - Just like in any other field, be it teaching, medical, or electrical, states control their own requirements and accept most school program credits and degrees, but there will be exceptions. Licensure is always a state requirement, with the state's own individual and national board exams. Although nearby states may have reciprocal exceptions this is not always the case. You can find out what your state requires through the Psychology Licensing Board in your state.

17. **Answer: D** - Victor Frankl is one of the primary therapists associated with the development of existentialism. He wrote "*Man's Search for Meaning*" and called his approach to treatment logo therapy- therapy through meaning. Born in Vienna, Austria in 1905, he was imprisoned in a Nazi prison camp during much of the Second World War

18. **Answer: A** - According to Gestalt therapists, people experience psychological difficulties because they have become cut off from important parts of themselves. *Gestalt* is defined as a structured entity that is more than the sum of its parts. The purpose of Gestalt therapy is to help people acknowledge important parts of themselves they have "cut off" such as emotions, bodies, or contact with others. Successful therapy creates awareness in the neglected and disowned parts and restores a sense of wholeness.

19. **Answer: C** - In order to supervise other counselors in their clinical work, a clinician must have specific credentials that vary from state to state. In each state, a certain amount of direct contact hours with clients are required. States vary the amount of these hours and type of licensure needed to supervise other counselors and their work with people.

20. **Answer: D** - Diversity training focuses on differences in people, whether it is demographics (age, gender, religious beliefs) or cultural differences. The purpose of diversity training is to create a greater understanding of cultures and belief systems in order to prevent miscommunication and misconceptions.

Cultural awareness assists the clinician to communicate effectively, verbally and nonverbally, and accurately interpret client body language and verbal cues. It also gives the clinician knowledge of subsystems within the culture (family, community, religion), which helps assess client concerns accurately.

21. **Answer: A** - In this situation, the counselor needs diversity training to effectively assist her client. Diversity training provides knowledge of differing cultures and insight into the cultural norms of a particular community. Knowledge of the importance of family, differences in frame of reference, and how mental health concerns are presented in a particular culture are all important pieces of diversity training. A degree in Asian culture is not necessary, nor is a recommendation from another therapist. An eagerness to assist the client would also be helpful, but diversity training is essential.

22. **Answer: D** - Each state determines the number of hours a counselor needs to be supervised prior to licensing, as well as how often they must meet with their supervisor. To check on this in your state, contact the licensing division on the state website. Usually the supervisor and counselor meet at least monthly, with the supervisor assisting and consulting with the clients being seen.

23. **Answer: B** - The counselor will need to receive consent to release information from the client in most states in order to discuss counseling progress with the supervisor. It is important for clients to realize the counselor is being supervised by a licensed clinician and what this entails for the client. It is not necessary for the client to know how often the counselor meets with the supervisor, although they might ask.

24. **Answer: D** - Stress management techniques and group facilitation are types of training that a lead clinician might provide for counselors under his supervision. Group facilitation is an important skill to learn and brush up on through the years, as counselors often lead groups in their practice. Stress management skills, for both the counselor to practice him/herself, or to teach to clients, are valuable skills as well. Wine tasting is best left to the personal preference of each counselor in their after work hours.

25. **Answer: B** - Culture awareness training addresses the cultural belief systems. Other topics that might be covered include style of communicating, world view of the culture (how life is seen as a whole), and other areas necessary for effective communication, understanding, and connection with a person from a particular culture. It may be of interest to know the geographical location of the culture of origin or their preferred foods, but perhaps not as vital to the counseling/client relationship.

26. **Answer: A** - By performing a data analysis of the research, the lead clinician can get an unbiased, research-based overview of EMDR as a method of treatment in clients. She may then observe the use of EMDR on clients and discuss the use of this method with the counselors to get a clear impression of the treatment within the organization.

27. **Answer: D** - Depending on the type of evaluation, a lead clinician might ask to sit in on a session with a client's permission or videotape the session for later viewing and skill development training. The lead clinician might also review client files for accuracy of paperwork and documented client progress. This decision would need to be made in respect to the client. If this would create discomfort and inhibit the counseling process, it may not be a viable option.

28. **Answer: C** - Quality assurance and control in a clinical practice ensures all client files are accurate and up-to-date, with all necessary legal documents filled out and signed, treatment plans completed and signed by client and clinician, assessments entered into the file, any testing results in place, progress or case notes accurate and up-to-date, and client's progress and any other clinical notes of concern documented. This may be done by the clinic supervisor, a team of counselors, or a quality assurance team member.

29. **Answer: D** - In a clinic, all three areas are important aspects of evaluation. The use of time management skills is a necessary component to managing the work load. If a counselor uses a large amount of time completing paperwork, there is either less time to see clients or the counselor is spending a large amount of overtime or personal time to complete the required case notes. Accurate and timely completion of paperwork is necessary to assure quality and to refresh the counselor's memory prior to the next counseling session. Progression toward client goals is a vital area of evaluation. Clients need to make progress and see progress toward their goals in the counseling process or soon become discouraged.

30. **Answer: D** - When a counselor is not making progress with a client, many options are available to help resolve the issue. Most likely, a consultation with other counselors in the practice, including the lead counselor, may engender additional insights and ideas to move the client toward progression. If consultation is not helpful, another counselor may be asked to observe a session and provide feedback. Usually, terminating a relationship with the client is not the answer, unless it is determined, through much discussion with client and lead clinician, that another counselor would be a better fit for the client and his/her concerns.

31. **Answer: D** - A lead clinician might decide to provide refresher training on a particular diagnosis if counselors see an increase in this type of disorder or he may address it at a weekly clinical meeting, asking for feedback and opening it up for group discussion. No other action may need to be taken other than an observation of the increase. The lead clinician might also look into a community awareness program highlighting this disorder.

32. **Answer: B** - A community needs assessment looks at the strengths and resources of a community in assisting its people in a variety of ways. The assessment might reveal plenty of health facilities, but a lack of transportation to get to the facilities. As needs are assessed, task forces may be created to address the issues of concern.

33. **Answer: D** - A director of a counseling practice might conduct or be a part of a community needs assessment both to ensure clinic services are providing for the community's mental health concerns, as well as assisting with the overall well-being of the community. The results of the assessment might determine offering additional services or replacing services not fully utilized with those that might be more needed.

34. **Answer: D** - Although a satellite office may be an expensive solution, it may be viable, depending on the need and size of the population. Less expensive solutions could include an outreach program, evening classes, or support groups held in local area churches or community buildings.

35. **Answer: D** -All of the options listed in this question are factors that determine the placement of new clients among counselors. It is important for a good fit between client and counselor to achieve a healthy therapeutic alliance. The presenting problem and the counselor's area of expertise might determine placement, as well as age and gender of client. Some female clients prefer seeing a female counselor; others may prefer a male counselor. A counselor's caseload may determine placement as well. Adding to an already full caseload can create counselor burn out and a decrease in client success.

36. **Answer: D** - A dual relationship is a concurrent relationship with a client. An example of such a relationship would be seeing a client who is also your accountant. This type of relationship is generally considered unethical. As a general rule, counselors should not engage in intimate relationships with clients, nor share social, activities, business dealings, or more other non-therapeutic interactions.

37. **Answer: C** - Research does not provide much information what demographic characteristics make an effective clinician. One interesting variable that has shown a correlation with outcome is the clinician's perception of having difficulties during their own childhood. It is unclear if the outcome is due to other factors during this period.

38. **Answer: D** - Confidentiality is an important aspect of the therapeutic relationship because it helps the clients feel safe in treatment and encourages them to share sensitive material. It helps the client trust the clinician, not the other way around. At the same time, confidentiality has limits; for clients who are minors, those who present a danger to themselves or others, or those who have abused a child, an elderly person, or a disabled person.

39.

Answer: B - Duty to warn is the duty to protect clients who present a danger to themselves or others. The decision to break confidentiality is not an easy one and should be made with extreme care; consult with a colleague or supervisor when faced with this issue.

40. **Answer: D** - Although an active social life might be enjoyable, as well as prevent stress, it is not one of the personal characteristics of an effective clinician. Having good interpersonal skills and qualities similar to what people most value in friends are characteristics that also make an effective clinician, such as being friendly and likeable, self-confident, healthy self-esteem, and the ability to affirm others rather than diminish them.

41. **Answer: C** - Clinicians choose approaches that are compatible with their personality styles. Erikson, the developmental psychologist, studied the relationship between a clinician's preferred theoretical orientations and personality types. Findings suggested that those clinicians who like to think chose cognitive styles of approach, while those who were feeling types chose more affective approaches.

42. **Answer: D** - Strategies that might be developed to address high levels of substance use in teens within your practice area include an effective public awareness campaign, a teen support group, or parenting classes. The director of outreach programming would need to evaluate the demographics and concerns in the area before choosing one or several of these approaches.

43. **Answer: A** - Active listening skills are very helpful to have when acting as a consultant to another counselor. Active listening skills are usually characterized by paying attention, nodding, rephrasing, asking an occasional question, and being a good sounding board for the person who is talking.

44. **Answer: A** - Ethics and values differ in that ethics dictate the boundaries of professional therapy, whereas values predict the stimulus and workings of therapy. Ethics is a person's governing body telling him or her what he or she can or cannot do. Values are a person's mind telling him or her what he or she should or should not do. A professional can abide by his or her code of ethics but still do things that are questionable.

45. **Answer: B** - If a counselor is aware that a client is engaging in illegal drug use, the counselor is not bound by law to notify the proper authorities or this activity. The counselor should only break confidentiality and notify the proper authorities if the client's activities will likely do harm to him or herself, another person, or property. Once a client trusts his or her counselor, the counselor might ask if he or she would like help with the drug issue. The counselor might cite health, financial, or legal reasons as incentive for the client to kick his or her habit.

46. **Answer: D** - The makeup of the counselor's community, the makeup of the client's community, and the client's culture are some issues every counselor must consider before making an ethical decision. Other issues might include the counselor's theoretical orientation and culture. Each client and counselor is unique, and the counselor must take care to treat each client as an individual.

47. **Answer: C** - It is important for a counselor to question him or herself as much, if not more, than he or she questions other counselors because questioning one's self is positive and productive, and will challenge the counselor to explore new avenues. Some counselors find it easier to question others than to question themselves. No one is perfect, mistakes can be made, or something can be overlooked. Questioning one's self can help avoid frequent mistakes.

48. **Answer: A** - Ethical alertness is an ongoing, progressive procedure that involves continual questioning and personal responsibility. Conflicts with insurance companies, the seriousness of clients' needs, and the possibility of lawsuits are just a few of the many things that can work to dull a counselor's sense of personal responsibility. A counselor can become overwhelmed, but it is imperative to exercise continual alertness in opting how to proceed in every step.

Fundamentals

1.

Answer: D - The Diagnostic and Statistical Manual of Mental Disorders (DSM-5) is a classification system developed by a task force of the American Psychiatric Association and is used to describe abnormal behaviors and determine mental related diagnosis.

2.

Answer: A - The DSM-5 does not attempt to explain the causes of disorders; it is strictly descriptive.

3.

Answer: C - There have been several editions of the DSM, starting with the first one in 1952, the second in 1968, the third in 1980, the revised third edition in 1987, and the fourth in 1994, and DSM-5 in 2013. In 2000, there was also a "text revision" version of the DSM-IV, DSM-IV-TR, was issued, which expanded information on each diagnosis and updated diagnostic codes to be consistent with the International Classification of Diseases coding system.

4.

Answer: D - The creators of the DSM keep releasing new editions of the manual to incorporate new information, to incorporate changes in the way abnormal behaviors are viewed, and to change the descriptions and categories. Scientific research on new disorders is ongoing, and information from this research needs to be added. Societal changes about the way we think of abnormal behaviors occur regularly, and these changes need to be reflected in the language of the manual. Finally, the list of disorders keeps expanding, creating a need for changes in the descriptions of disorders and the categorization of disorders.

5.

Answer: B - The DSM-5 classifies disorders that people have, not the people themselves. The text in the DSM-5 avoids the use of terms such as "schizophrenia." Instead, it uses the more awkward, but accurate, term "a person with schizophrenia."

6. **Answer: A** - Insanity is a legal term. It indicates that a person cannot be held responsible for his/her actions because of mental illness.

7.

Answer: A - The statement is true. Eighteen years after the DSM-IV came out, the authors revised it to help with the many changes in the 18 years between the release and the revision. However, it was still the same edition, IV, of the DSM. The DSM-5 was just released 2013.

8. **Answer: B** - Age appears to be unrelated to outcome in therapeutic treatment. However, intelligence, education, and socioeconomic level all have an impact on successful outcome of treatment. In most treatment modalities, thinking skills, the ability to look at current and past behaviors, and to adapt during treatment are all important parts of the success of the outcome and with limited intelligence, this would be difficult. Education levels again would have an effect on many modalities depending on types of treatment uses. Socioeconomic level may indicate other variables affecting outcome (i.e., transportation issues, payment, and cultural norms for entering therapy, to name a few).

9. **Answer: D** - The question "why did you drink so much?" has an accusatory ring to it and can put the client on the defensive, closing down any further communication between client and clinician. "How did you feel about that" elicits the client's feelings about her actions and is nonjudgmental, likely leading to an exploration of her feelings behind the action of drinking excessively. "What happened?" is a general question asking for clarification and the client would go on with her narrative, perhaps giving background information and leading to more discussion. "What would you do differently next time?" allows the client to see drinking excessively as a behavior she can choose or not choose and would again lead to further conversation and insight into the behavior.

10. **Answer: B** - Clients with psychotic disorders are most likely to lack the ability to engage in the self-examination required by Adlerian theory. In depth self-examination requires logic, good cognitive functioning, and the ability to be free from hallucinations and other psychotic events. Impulse control and personality and anxiety disorders do not affect the ability to be present and focused on the tasks the Adlerian clinician asks the client to complete.

11. **Answer: C** - The question "did you have a good week?" is not an open question. It allows the person to answer in a closed way, either yes or no, without giving any additional information and is thus not a good way to elicit information in an interview with a client. "What brought you here," "how are things going," and "how did you react" all require the client to answer in greater detail and brings in a depth to the interview.

12. **Answer: D** - People who are highly motivated, pragmatic, logical, fairly resilient, and tough-minded do well with REBT (Rational Emotive Behavior Therapy). This modality is a direct, somewhat confrontational approach to therapy.

13. **Answer: D** - A clinician can create a therapeutic alliance with their client by mutuality, genuineness, and hope. Mutuality is a feeling of shared warmth, affection, affirmation, and respect. Genuineness is giving the client clear, accurate, and honest yet sensitive messages. Having hope throughout the therapeutic process enables clients to persist in the hard work, i.e. therapy.

14. **Answer: C** - The working alliance focuses on shared goals and an agreement to engage in certain tasks to achieve those goals. Transpersonal relationships communicate to the client the sense of therapy as a shared journey leading to personal growth. I-You relationships emphasize immediacy and mutuality in the therapeutic relationship, with the clinician serving as a role model. Reparative relationships are most often used with severely damaged clients and offers re-parenting and nurturing in an effort to compensate for deprivation in an earlier relationship.

15. **Answer: B** - Role induction is the process of familiarizing the client with the nature of counseling, their responsibilities in this collaborative process, and the kinds of changes that can realistically be expected from treatment. This undertaking can help both client and clinician view each other as engaged in a common endeavor that is likely to succeed.

16. **Answer: D** - Duty to warn a client when the therapist will be on vacation is not part of the professional definition of duty to warn. Duty to warn is the directive to protect clients and others from physical, mental, or emotional harm and in fulfilling those duties, a clinician may sometimes need to break confidentiality in order to report their concerns to those needing to know in order to prevent harm. As the decision to break confidentiality is usually an extremely difficult one to make due to the therapeutic alliance with the client, clinicians are encouraged to seek consultation with a colleague or a supervisor.

17. **Answer: A** - Two personal characteristics of the effective clinician are friendly and likeable. Additionally, being patient, flexible, having a sense of humor, a realistic self-confidence, self-esteem, and being motivated toward personal and professional growth also lead to success in clinical work.

18. **Answer: D** - All of the choices listed in this questions is a critical components of the diagnostic interview. Diagnostic interviews vary in length and content, but all include a family and social history, a medical background, and a list of previous diagnoses, if any. From there, depending on the type of clinician, other elements will be added, including current symptoms, lifestyle questions, drug use, etc.

19. **Answer: D** - Clinicians need to refer clients to a health professional when a possible underlying medical condition is discovered or when additional concerns discovered are not within the clinician's expertise. Also, perhaps an underlying substance abuse issue has been disclosed and the client would benefit from attending a support group; referral to an appropriate agency or community group might be given.

20. **Answer: D** - All of the options listed are part of the GAF. Each 10 points on the scale shows a point of function for the adult, ranging from the persistent danger of suicide or hurting others (1-10), to an extremely well-functioning individual (91-100). Professionals use their subjective opinion on interviewing to assess the client's ability to function and give this client a rating using this scale.

21. **Answer: B** - Referring to the initial treatment plan where treatment goals were determined is an excellent way to assess a client's progress toward those goals. Is treatment on track or has therapy taken on a life of its own and wandered away from the initial treatment goals? A clinician might discuss these goals and progress towards them with the client as part of the therapeutic process, but would first refer to the treatment plan. Remember confidentiality.

22. **Answer: D** - The BDI, or Beck Depression Inventory, is a reliable, valid test for assessing depression. It has been extensively studied for content validity, concurrent validity, and construct validity. The MMPI-Tis an empirically-based assessment of adult psychopathology. The QOLI is a quality of life inventory. The HTP, or the house-tree-person projective drawing technique, was designed to aid clinicians in obtaining information concerning an individual's sensitivity, maturity, flexibility, efficiency, degree of personality integration, and interaction with the environment.

23. **Answer: D** - All of the above are ways the MBHI can be useful to help identify possible psychosomatic complications, help predict response to illness or treatment, help in the development of effective rehabilitation programs, or for those who have problems that may stem from a psychological disorder or an unidentified stressor.

24. **Answer: A** - In children, symptoms of bipolar disorder can be very similar to Attention Deficit Hyperactivity Disorder (ADHD). For a child to be appropriately diagnosed, the clinician needs to listen carefully to the parental history of the child's actions and behaviors in addition to utilizing assessments designed for children, not adults.

25. **Answer: D** - Acquiring insight and new understanding into the self, as well as developing new perceptions or views to one's problems are both common factors in effective treatment. Additional factors associated with client change are a belief that change is necessary and warmth and support from another person. Enjoying the process of counseling is not an indicator or factor in effective treatment.

26. **Answer: C** - Small behavioral changes leading to larger changes that have ripple effects on the whole system is the underlying theory of Brief Solution-Based therapy. Answer A is the underlying theory of Brief Psychodynamic psychotherapy. Answer B is the underlying theory of Person-Centered therapy and answer D is the underlying theory for Reality therapy.

27.

Answer: C - The criteria of Axis IV were modified and included in the DSM-5 as psychosocial and other contextual issues with significant bearing on the well-being of the patient. Axes I and III were folded in with Axis II in the list of disorders. Axis V was dropped completely.

28.

Answer: D - Antisocial, Borderline, and Nacissistic Personality Disorders are all Cluster B personality disorders, also known as dramatic personality disorders. Cluster A encompasses different types of schizophrenic disorders, and Cluster C covers personality disorders characterized by anxiety or fear.

29.

Answer: D - All of the choices listed in this question should be included as important contextual factors. Job loss, educational problems, and housing problems are all environmental concerns that a clinician would report in this section. Additional problems that could be listed might be problems with the primary support group, legal issues, and economic concerns.

30. **Answer: B** - A clinician starts at the top level of the GAF scale and keeps moving down the scale until the best match for the individual's function is located. To determine the specific rating within the ten point range, a clinician can consider whether the person is functioning at the lower or higher end of that range.

31.

Answer: C - Pervasive Developmental Disorder is one of several differential diagnoses for Reactive Attachment Disorder in children. Other possible diagnoses include Mental Retardation, Attention-Deficit/Hyperactivity Disorder, and Disruptive Behavior Disorders. Schizophrenia, Depression, and Anxiety are not part of a differential diagnosis for RAD.

32. **Answer: B** - The client's statement is an example of overgeneralization. Overgeneralization occurs when a person draws sweeping conclusions that are not justified by the evidence, as in the case of this statement. It is similar to all-or-nothing thinking, which is viewing a situation in terms of extremes such as "either I am completely good or completely bad. Catastrophizing is predicting a negative outcome without considering other possibilities and disqualifying the positive focuses on only negative information, ignoring any positive input.

33. **Answer: C** - Activity scheduling is used by clinicians to elicit new cognitions in their clients by giving people the opportunity to try out new behaviors and ways of thinking. It encourages them to remain active despite feelings of sadness or apprehension. Learning a new and interesting skill and having a good time can contribute to improved moods and clearer thinking. So perhaps snow-skiing or skydiving might be one of the activities scheduled!

34. **Answer: B** - Cognitive therapists might assign a person self-talk if they have low self-esteem or are used to hearing many negative messages, either externally or internally. Self-talk is closely related to affirmations, which is sort of a slogan that is positive and reinforcing. People can post these wherever they might be often seen, such as on the refrigerator or bathroom mirror.

35. **Answer: A** - The primary purpose of a strengths- based assessment is to focus on the strengths, accomplishments, achievements, talents, and uniqueness of a client. This not only enhances the client/clinician relationship, but also allows the client to hope for the possibility of change within themselves and/or their situation. A belief in the client and their strengths is essential for a true, strengths-based assessment.

36. **Answer: B** - Conceptualization is the first phase in SIT training. The client and therapist develop a collaborative relationship and the client is taught about the nature of stress. The client's thoughts on stress and past experiences with stressful situations are explored in depth. Skills Acquisition is the next phase where coping skills are taught and is followed by Application and Follow-through; the third phase in SIT training.

37. **Answer: B** - When using *anchoring* in treatment with a client, the clinician is attempting to create planned positive responses to certain situations. Positive *anchors* can be created to help people reach their goals. Anchors can be planned or spontaneous, positive or negative, external or internal. An example of a positive, spontaneous, external anchor might be the smell of freshly baked cookies, which reminds the person of their grandma who used to bake cookies whenever they visited her. Anchors can occur in any of the sensory channels and can be used to promote positive responses.

38. **Answer: C** - Cognitive therapy is based on the finding that changes in thinking lead to changes in feeling and acting. These changes occur when a client and clinician develop a positive therapeutic alliance and focus on the present, although attention is paid to the past when it is indicated. Cognitive therapy uses a broad range of techniques and interventions to help people evaluate and change their cognitions.

39. **Answer: A** - Maturity and the capacity for relationships are two characteristics of a successful client. Clients who are mature are likely to make a commitment to treatment and follow through on task assignments. The capacity for relationships is an ability to invest energy and caring in personal relationships and have trust in others.

40. **Answer: D** - While many of the other skills listed are useful, having respect for the client, optimism in seeking a realistic solution, and excellent communication skills are essential for a skilled clinician. Respecting the client through verbal and nonverbal communication, for their value and belief systems, and for their strengths are all underlying traits that set the foundation for good clinical work. Sharing optimism with the client (even when the work is difficult) that a realistic solution will be reached gives the client the strength needed to continue.

41.

Answer: C - A markedly diminished interest or pleasure in most all activities nearly every day for two weeks is a necessary symptom for a diagnosis of a Major Depressive Episode. Such a diagnosis can be made when this symptom is also accompanied by other symptoms of depression for a total of five or more symptoms.

42. **Answer: B** - ADHD is still the leading diagnosed disorder in children, with boys four times more likely to receive the diagnosis than girls. The majority of children are not diagnosed with this disorder until school-age; most likely because of the greater confinements of sitting in a desk and paying attention for longer periods of time.

43. **Answer: D** - The Dyadic Trust Scale is an eight-item questionnaire that takes less than three minutes to fill out and focuses on the level of trust between marriage partners. Trust is seen as an important aspect in marital harmony and is usually defined as the belief in one person of the level of integrity in another.

44. **Answer: D** - In single parent families created by divorce, stressors for custodial parents finances, social life, and parenting alone. Child care concerns, co-parenting, and visitation rights also create stress on the custodial parent and the family.

45. **Answer: D** - Elderly couples are concerned about finances, physical health of each other, and possible memory loss. They may also be concerned about being left alone when one spouse dies, needing additional care and leaving their home and neighborhood, and being able to remain as independent as possible.

46. **Answer: B** - Learning to share with a partner is one of the major early tasks of a new couple. Developing personal autonomy is usually learned when a person leaves home for the first time, perhaps going to college or getting their first apartment, and developing a support group needs to be addressed whenever a person moves. Adjusting to decreased energy is usually a task for new parents.

47. **Answer: D** - Informed consent is a "contract" between the clinician and the client, brought out and discussed in the first session, outlining both clinician and client responsibilities to the therapeutic process. Informed consent forms may vary from clinician to clinician, but usually include information about confidentiality, duty to warn, the clinician's approach to therapy, and other "housekeeping" duties such as scheduling, after hours information, etc. Client responsibilities may include keeping appointments, agreeing to do assignments, or other elements the clinician believes are important enough to put in writing.

48. **Answer: B** - One likely reason why a clinician would end seeing a client is that he or she is experiencing life changes such as retiring from practice or leaving the agency. These decisions are not made lightly and usually engender a great deal of planning on the part of the clinician and the agency.

49. **Answer: A** - Usually, termination by mutual agreement occurs when clients and clinicians both believe that a client has made good progress toward goals and is ready to stop treatment, at least temporarily. Occasionally, clients and clinicians may both agree that treatment is not working and that a client would be more likely to benefit from another clinician or approach to treatment.

Group Work

1. **Answer: B** - A 'norm' is an expected behavior that is adhered to by members of the group. Norms are society's definition of how we "should" behave. These norms differ from culture to culture and also from group to group within each culture.

2. **Answer: C** - Conforming to group pressure because of a need of acceptance and approval is referred to as Normative Social Influence. This could range from doing things such as asking what everyone is wearing to a certain social function to giving in to destructive or illegal behaviors to maintain acceptance and approval.

3. **Answer: D** - The comfortable distance to maintain between people is known as Personal Space. This distance will vary from culture to culture. For instance, Americans seem to like twice as much distance as say, the Chinese culture. The preferred interpersonal distance will differ according to the situation also.

4. **Answer: A** - The phenomenon described in this question is Informational Social Influence. Have you ever bought a specific brand of product (a cell phone, or ski equipment) because your friend recommended it? You conform not to gain their approval (Normative Social Influence), but because you assume they have more information or experience in the matter than you do. That is Informational Social Influence.

5. **Answer: B** - Anyone we admire, like, or want to imitate is in our Reference Group. A funny thing about humans is that we think if we just wear the same kind of outfit, or use the same makeup, or buy the same type of sports shoes, we will be just as gorgeous, athletic, or as talented as our favorite star or personage.

6. **Answer: C** - Conformity and obedience are the two major forms of social influence. When people understand all the factors involved in a situation they can use that knowledge to decide when obedience and/or conformity is appropriate and ethical. Conformity and obedience in the wrong group or portion of society can also be a major influence in the downfall of society.

7. **Answer: D** - Research has found that when participants are reminded that they will be held responsible for an outcome (harm to others, destruction of property, et cetera), destructive obedience is reduced sharply. Responsibility reminders in all actions help participants make their 'own' decisions instead of 'group' decisions.

8. **Answer: D** - All of the descriptions in this question fit conformity. When you conform (or change) your opinions, actions, or thinking to fit into or belong to a group of any size (remember two can be a group), you are giving in to 'conformity.'

9. **Answer: D** - Consistency and consensus are the two criteria listed in this question (the third is distinctiveness). When all three are high, Harold Kelly says we tend to make external attributions, but when consensus and distinctiveness are low and consistency is high, we tend to make internal attributions.

10. **Answer: A** - Saliency bias is the tendency to focus attention on vivid (salient) or more noticeable factors when explaining the causes of behavior. The fact that the more noticeable factors out show the situational factors help us to make quicker judgments. This leads to another factor called "blaming the victim."

11. **Answer: D** - All of the choices in this question are reasons that people are likely to blame the victim. An example of blaming the victim that is often used is one of blaming people on welfare for their joblessness or asking people who have been victimized by poverty, robbery, or rape 'why' they got themselves into such a situation. Again, it's the most noticeable, stand out factor that we see first, so we tend to affix blame without looking into the situational factors that are not concrete and conspicuous. Or we use the 'blanketing' effect-if a few incidences of people cheating the welfare system are made known, for example, we just assume that all people receiving welfare are guilty of something like it.

12. **Answer: C** - The appeal must engender a lot of fear, the audience must believe the message, and specific instructions for avoiding the danger must be presented. Fear induction can come from all kinds of sources - from politicians warning us of higher taxes and more crime if we don't vote for them, to ads warning us of social rejection if we don't use the right mouthwash, or on a more serious note, a public service announcement about drinking and driving. With these three factors in any message, it is likely to be received as 'truth' by someone.

13. **Answer: D** - Resistance is not a factor. Reactance is a phenomenon in which people increase their resistance to persuasion when feel pressured. Personality traits, involvement, and vulnerability are the other three characteristics.

14. **Answer: D** - All of the choices in this question describe in-group favoritism and out-group negativity. An in-group is any category in which people see themselves as a member, while the out-group consists of all others. People see their In-group members in a better light than "all the others." In other words, they cognitively practice in-group favoritism and out-group negativity.

15. **Answer: B** - The "they all look alike to me" tendency is termed Out-group Homogeneity Effect. When members of minority groups are not perceived as varied and complex, individuals who have the same needs and feelings as the dominant group find it easier to perceive the members of the minority groups as faceless objects, thus treating them as less than human.

16. **Answer: D** - All of the choices listed are reasons for the aggression to be displaced. If the target of your aggression were bigger, stronger, and could cause much more harm than it is causing at present, wouldn't you pick on a lesser combatant? Sometimes governments, a much larger group, or a bigger bully is just more than one small group or human can handle. The chosen lesser target is known as the 'scapegoat.'

17. **Answer: C** - Super ordinate goals are one of the methods to combat prejudice and aggression between groups. One of the ways researchers have found to combat prejudice and aggression between groups is to give both groups a common goal that is higher than individual goals and is a benefit to both groups. A common goal should take cooperative efforts on both sides to obtain, put both groups on an equal basis, and give equal benefits to both sides.

18. **Answer: D** - Prejudice is an attitude, but discrimination refers to negative behavior directed at members of a group. Discrimination often results from prejudice, but not always. People do not always act on their prejudices.

19. **Answer: A** - Learning and individual personality needs are both sources of prejudice. The other three major factors that are the most commonly cited sources of prejudice are processes, economic/political competition, and displaced aggression.

20. **Answer: C** - The most common forms of group therapy include family therapy, support groups, and encounter groups. Group therapy started as an economic form of therapy and has become a preferred approach in many instances.

21. **Answer: A** - The family is seen as an interrelated system in which each member has a major role. When families first come into therapy, many believe that one member is *the* cause of all their problems. It is usually necessary to change ways of interacting within the family system.

22. **Answer: B** - The object of family therapy is to restore family relationships. Family therapy can also accomplish a number of other things such as growth of family members and the family as a whole. It can also serve as a family intervention.

23. **Answer: D** - All of the choices listed in this question are helpful factors of support groups. During times of stress and emotional trouble, it is easy to imagine we are alone and our troubles unique. Knowing that others have similar problems can be very reassuring. And seeing others improve can give us hope and motivation to improve our own situation.

24. **Answer: C** - Reasons to join a support group include life crises, destructive behaviors, and new life challenges. The mutual support for shared problems, the feedback information, and the behavioral rehearsals can all be very helpful.

25. **Answer: D** - Encounter groups promote personal growth and interpersonal communication by encouraging participants to openly share emotion, to tell it like it is to each other, and to have intense confrontations. These groups are not for the faint of heart. Everything is out front and open, this includes tearing down one another's defenses, openly sharing emotions, and talking straight with one another. This type of group is not for people who are seriously disturbed.

26. **Answer: B** - The biggest potential problem with group therapy is that the group leader may not be well trained/experienced enough. In such therapy, the group leader has major responsibilities. If he or she is not well trained and experienced the interactions could become psychologically harmful.

27. **Answer: C** - The most helpful aspect of group therapy is hearing similar comments from several group members concerning your problem or behavior. When a group member receives similar comments about his/her behavior or situation from several members of the group, the message may be more convincing than if it comes from a single therapist.

28. **Answer: D** - A role in a group is a set of behavioral patterns defined by a category of people. Every person in a group is expected to play one or more roles. Such a role might be a police officer or a president of a club.

29. **Answer: B** - Some roles are regulated and spelled out (such as a police officer), whereas others are assumed through informal learning and inference, such as a mother or father.

30. **Answer: A** - Roles affect behavior significantly. Have you ever observed people you know as they 'take on' a different role? As an everyday Mom takes on her role as a classroom teacher, how does her demeanor change? As a neighbor, who's an ordinary guy, takes on his role as the chairman over a cub scout meeting, what changes about him? Are you different with certain friends than you are with others?

31. **Answer: C** - Deindividuation occurs when individuals temporarily suspend their normal identity in a group setting. You get caught up in the group action and go along with things you would never do on your own. An individual becomes less aware of his own values and becomes more sensitive to the group's actions and desires. Think of gang activities such as the actions of the Ku Klux Klan.

32. **Answer: D** - Groupthink is a condition in which a highly cohesive group with a strong desire for agreement avoids inconsistent information. This decision-making strategy can lead to poor choices. It could be a family, a panel of advisors, or an athletic team.

33.

Answer: D - Group polarization generally occurs when a group decision becomes more conservative or more risky. This situation occurs when a group initially makes a decision, discusses it, and then moves in a more extreme direction (either more conservative or more risky) than the initial decision.

34. **Answer: C** - Anytime two or more people are interacting with one another and are influenced by each other, they are considered a group.

35. **Answer: D** - Peer-to-peer support, counseling referrals, and surviving seminars are some of the many kinds of support that groups offer to those who are grieving the loss of a loved one. Coping with the death of a spouse is a difficult situation; there are many support groups to help those grieving such a situation. Military families receive bereavement support through the Tragedy Assistance Program for Survivors (T.A.P.S.); just one of many groups that offers peer-to-peer support, counseling referrals, survivor seminars, and other types of help.

36. **Answer: A** - Group counseling during the grieving process can help a person realize he is not alone and give a person the opportunity to learn from others. The grieving process can be a lonely, detached time in one's life, so having others around them that have gone, or are going, through the same feelings will help them to not feel so alone. It is also a good time to learn a few specific things that have helped others deal with these feelings and situations.

37. **Answer: C** - Groups for those who have experienced the loss of a child are another special loss group. The Bereaved Families of Ontario (BFO) and The Compassionate Friends are examples of such groups. BFO also provides assistance to children, adolescents, and young adults who lose a parent or sibling. The grieving for different members of the family presents different dynamics for those doing the grieving.

38. **Answer: A** - Sometimes groups are facilitated by a trained professional; others are composed of only peers. Peer-to-peer groups are very helpful in all areas of counseling. We seem to be more open to our peers and their experiences and solutions. And who could possibly be more understanding, in tune with us, or more encouraging than peers who have gone through the same ordeal and survived?

39. **Answer: B** - The feedback and support from both the clinician and the group members can accelerate the process of awareness and empowerment. Members can also learn vicariously from each other. Listening to one person in the group express thoughts and feelings can lead to insight in another member in the group.

40. **Answer: C** - Fritz Perls's work at the Esalen Institute emphasized the use of the Hot Seat in a group setting. The Hot Seat is a powerful technique utilized in gestalt therapy in group settings. The hot seat is a chair placed in the middle of the group, usually with a box of tissues nearby since sitting in the hot seat often evokes strong emotions. Group members volunteer to work, one at a time, spending 5-10 minutes sitting in the hot seat and becoming the center of the group's attention.

41. **Answer: B** - In the Gestalt group technique known as Making the Rounds, group members listen while the person in the hot seat says something to each member of the group, perhaps identifying something she wants from that person or something in her that reminds her of herself. The group members might give feedback to the person in the hot seat, perhaps on her strengths in an effort to empower her.

42. **Answer: B** - Participants in REBT group therapy have the opportunity to observe and try out behaviors, as well as share feedback and reactions. Group members are encouraged to take responsibility for helping each other as well as themselves.

43. **Answer: C** - While REBT can be very well-suited for treatment in a group setting, it is not appropriate for people who have psychotic disorders, who are highly suicidal or fragile, or who have other severe mental disorders. It is also not recommended for people who have had traumatic childhood experiences or problems with impulse control and substance use.

44. **Answer: D** - When providing group counseling, a clinician should be knowledgeable about member selection and member and leadership roles in groups, as well as familiar with systems and strategies of group counseling. A clinician needs to be knowledgeable about member selection, as group dynamics will play a big part in the effectiveness of the work done within its parameters. With this in mind, a thorough grounding in the group counseling strategies and systems can assist groups in overcoming obstacles.

45. **Answer: A** - Sitting in the hot seat is a technique created by Gestalt therapist, Fritz Perls, which allows group members to become the focus of the group for 5-10 minutes, talking to and receiving feedback from members of the group.

46. **Answer: C** - CBGT is very effective for people with anxiety disorders. Working within the group provides clients an opportunity to practice their cognitive restructuring skills and experience success in a safe and controlled environment. Positive group feedback for the efforts made create empowerment, not only for the person, but for all members of the group.

47. **Answer: D** - Stress management, anger management, and social skills training can be taught in a group setting. The broader concept of group therapy can be taken to include any helping process that takes place in a group, including skills training groups. These types of groups are called psycho educational groups and are open to any in the population seeking to benefit from learning these skills.

48. **Answer: A** - Group psychotherapy brings together people who have similar concerns and assists them in identifying maladaptive behaviors within a supportive structure. Group members also solve emotional difficulties through receiving feedback, direction, and support from both the clinician and the group members.

49. **Answer: C** - There have been documented cases of group psychotherapy leading to a worsening of present symptoms or an appearance of new symptoms. This style of psychotherapy, while benefiting some, appears to have a negative effect on others. More studies need to be completed to further assess the reasons behind the negative effects.

50. **Answer: B** - A key belief of group therapy is that although many clients experience emotional pain alone, they can get better when interacting with others facing similar problems. Group work centers on crucial life skills such as going through life in an innovative manner. This has been successful in the treatment of a number of sensitive and everyday living issues.

Human Growth and Development

1. **Answer: C** - Concrete operational thinking, occurring between ages 7-11, is the ability to solve problems, perform multiple classification tasks, and order objects in a logical sequence. Jean Piaget, a developmental biologist, studied intellectual development. His studies led him to understand that children are not little adults. The brain does not fully develop until after age 15. This led to his stages of cognitive development.

2. **Answer: B** - The stage of development titled Identity vs. Role Confusion begins in the teen years according to Erik Erikson. According to Erikson, social development progresses through eight stages and creates what is called a "psychosocial crisis" that must be resolved successfully before moving on to the next stage. In teens, this crisis is Identity vs. role confusion and is based on the question *Who am I?* This stage can last up to age 20. Self-doubt is a normal part of the process, as is taking on a variety of roles in the search for identity.

3. **Answer: C** - The social relationships perspective includes the ability to recognize good and bad intentions in one's self. This is seen in stage three (interpersonal accord and conformity driven) of Kohlberg's theory. Individuals are receptive to approval or disapproval from others as it reflects society's accordance with the perceived role.

4. **Answer: A** - Personality is the consistent and unique pattern of social and emotional behavior that defines an individual. Self-actualization is part of Maslow's theory of personality development.

5.

Answer: B - Caring for others is the focus of the psychosocial theory of development. In every stage of development, the ability to connect and care for others is an essential component.

6. **Answer: A** - The selective way we recall our personal histories is one possible reason for the gap adults experience between their present view of themselves and their memories of childhood. Neurologic research on memory encoding suggests memories are stored differently as children than as adults, leading to the possible gap in the way we see ourselves and our past.

7. **Answer: B** - During old age, people experience the crisis of ego integrity vs. despair according to Erikson. Integrity is achieved if the prior stages have been resolved successfully and the mature person is able to trust, is independent, and looks forward to new experiences and looks back with satisfaction. If prior stages are not resolved, the person might view his/her life with despair, feeling like they have failed or fallen short in life.

8. **Answer: C** - While all of the answers might be plausible, adolescence is defined as the period from the onset of puberty or sexual maturity to adulthood.

9. **Answer: D** - According to Erikson, Lucy has entered the stage of autonomy vs. shame and doubt, which may involve a stormy time of the expression of will, including tantrums and stubbornness. Resolved successfully, Lucy will emerge from this stage with self-confidence, a better ability to control herself, and ready to learn more about the world around her.

10. **Answer: A** - The context becomes the most important element in problem solving to the adult, as they are able to see the complexities of issues surrounding the problem. While the problem itself and its solution are important, the context in which the problem exists is more of the focus for an adult thinker. Children, as concrete thinkers, can only focus on the problem and can likely see only one solution. It is later in life that abstract thinking occurs and the adult is able to see multiple solutions to one problem.

11. **Answer: B** - A strong need for activity is not typically one of the symptoms of bereavement. Many grieving people experience a loss of sleep and appetite, an empty feeling inside, and tightness in the throat. They may also experience a feeling of lethargy, an inability to act, and feeling as though they are moving in slow motion.

12. **Answer: D** - Carl Jung believed that personality does change when we age and is an important part of the aging process. Jungian analytical psychology is often thought of as a method for achieving personal growth and self-awareness and involves long-term psychoanalysis.

13. **Answer: B** - Paul Baltes' selective optimization with compensation theory best describes Mrs. Smith's improvement in some areas of her intellectual abilities and a decline in others. His lifespan development theory states that development is life-long, that it includes both losses and gains, and it is influenced by a historical, as well as cultural context.

14. **Answer: A** - According to Dan P. McAdams's studies of moral psychology, generativity is defined as centering our life goals more around doing for others as we age due to the desire to create purpose from life.

15. **Answer: C** - Recent retirement is not one of the warning signs for increased risk of committing suicide in an older depressed male, while the other signs (being socially isolated, over age 85, or becoming disabled by a chronic health problem) are all definite indicators of an increased risk of suicidality.

16. **Answer: C** - Our biological maleness or femaleness is called sex, whereas the psychosocial concept of our maleness or femaleness is called gender. Androgyny is the term indicating a mixing of traditional female and male traits, while chromosomal sex is the biological determination of either XX chromosomes (female) or XY chromosomes (male).

17. **Answer: B** - Erik Erikson's trust versus mistrust stage in the psychosocial development theory would support this direction to respond to an infant's cries in a timely manner in order to create trust. If infant's cries are not met with parental care and concern, the infant soon learns that his or her needs will not be met, creating a deep-seated feeling of mistrust.

18. **Answer: B** - This theory is known as the socio-cultural perspective of development. According to Vygotsky's theory, children can do more with the help and guidance of an adult or other more experienced person than they can do by themselves. Skinner's work supports the behavioral perspective; Freud's work supports the psychoanalytic perspective; and Piaget's work supports the intellectual aspects of development.

19. **Answer: C** - Symbolic representation is not one of Bandura's basic concepts in his social cognitive theory. Observational learning, self-efficacy, and reciprocal determination are all part of the cognitive thought processes that influence human behavior and functioning according to Bandura's social-cognitive approach. Simply put, his theory states that learning can occur simply through observation of models and in the absence of reinforcement.

20. **Answer: B** - Jean Piaget was one of the first developmental psychologists to examine how children think and reason. From ages 2-7, the preoperational stage of development, children can use mental representation to think and are now capable of symbolic representation - using a symbol to represent an object. Because of this, children learn language, which is a system of symbols.

21. **Answer: A** - A counselor of cultures different from his/her own needs to do additional research to be better able to understand the client's needs. Several culture-bound and culture-general symptoms that are useful in diagnosing disorders have been found. Also, it has become apparent that people learn to express their problems in ways acceptable to others in the same culture.

22. **Answer: D** - Besides the physical, hormonal, and social differences, males and females have been taught to express - or not to express - feelings, symptoms, and complaints in very different ways. Counseling someone of the opposite gender requires the counselor to think and respond differently to achieve the same goal.

23. **Answer: B** - In other cultures, we find that concepts of person and self are cultural constructions. Many cultures view a person primarily by looking at his or her place in the social unit. Western theories are heavily biased toward their perception of the independent self. Even within individualistic cultures (U.S. and Western Europe) women and minorities are likely to see themselves as more intricately connected with others. This not only explains why some theories may not apply to all groups, it also encourages research across cultures.

24. **Answer: A** - There have been 12 culture-general symptoms listed. Some of the above may be listed in the 12 generals, but a feeling of fullness in the head, problems with memory, and shortness of breath are three cultural-bound symptoms of note. There have been several research studies made on culture-bound disorders.

25. **Answer: C** - Victim of witchcraft is a culturally specific symptom of schizophrenia. Being possessed by evil spirits is also a cultural symptom. In the United States, the same experience (hearing voices) may occur in schizophrenia, but they may not be labeled as 'evil spirits' per se.

26. **Answer: B** - Research in industrialized nations shows that the rate of clinical (severe) depression for women is two to three times higher than the rate for men. Some researchers say the covariance between hormones and serotonin may explain gender differences in depression.

27. **Answer: D** - Meeting with people from another culture without knowing anything about that culture is always like trying to walk across an unknown river: you're more likely than not to end up in over your head! Before encountering people from a different culture, research into that culture is an absolute necessity. Seemingly small differences could be very important.

28. **Answer: C** - Becoming aware of your own cultural rules helps you to understand the differences, so you can become aware of your own thought processes. Adjust your behaviors to theirs. For instance, if you do not speak the language, get an interpreter and at least apologize for not speaking their language. It is frustrating not to be able to easily communicate with others and stressful not to find familiar ways of behaving.

29. **Answer: D** - A culturally specific approach to counseling involves familiarity with the cultural heritage, how the culture adjusts and manifests its reactions to power systems within its families, knowledge of culture percepts of society, and the ability to view problems within the context of the environment.

30. **Answer: D** - Essential traits of a multicultural counselor are a self-awareness and understanding of one's cultural history and experiences, comprehension of one's environmental experiences in mainstream culture, and perceptual sensitivity towards one's personal beliefs and values.

31. **Answer: A** - In addition to understanding the client's cultural history, having sensitivity toward the client's values and beliefs is an essential trait of a multicultural counselor. Being of the same culture is ideal, but trained counselors are not always available from a particular culture. Also, goodness of fit with a counselor may not be an issue if the client and counselor are from a different culture, as long as the counselor has good skills as a multicultural clinician.

32. **Answer: C** - The process of becoming a culturally skilled clinician is an active process that requires ongoing education and recognition that each culture is complex and diverse. As a clinician, it is essential to acknowledge our own personal limitations and to remain aware of our cultural biases.

33. **Answer: D** - A clinician can ask him/herself if they have an accurate understanding of the client's cultural normal and values. This knowledge can prevent misunderstandings and help guide the clinician in assisting the client in ways that are therapeutically helpful. Being aware of our own worldview, acknowledging we may hold stereotyped information about certain cultures, and examining this when beginning work with a client ensures these thoughts/beliefs do not create misunderstanding and barriers to the counseling process.

34. **Answer: B** - Culturally skilled clinicians are able to engage in a variety of verbal and nonverbal helping responses. When working with clients of a different ethnicity, clinicians understand and are able to send and receive both verbal and nonverbal messages accurately and appropriately, recognizing that helping styles and approaches may be culture bound.

35. **Answer: A** - Culturally skilled clinicians will understand that religious and/or spiritual beliefs and values will affect the worldview of the client, as well as their psychosocial functioning and how they express distress.

36. **Answer: C** - Self-awareness begins with asking questions about yourself, your culture, your belief systems, your values, and how these might affect your counseling skills. Honesty is the first step toward becoming a culturally skilled counselor.

37. **Answer: B** - People from non-western cultures may be uncomfortable with BPT because of the probing, interpretation, and exploration of early childhood issues that are a part of most versions of this type of therapy.

38. **Answer: B** - In many cultures, sharing thoughts is more comfortable than sharing emotions and cognitive therapy focuses on learning to think clearly and cope with life challenges. Because the cognitive therapy approach is respectful, addresses present concerns, and does not require disclosure of emotions and experiences that may be very personal, it is likely to appeal to people form a wide variety of cultural backgrounds.

39. **Answer: C** - Gestalt therapy may be uncomfortable for some populations because it tends to be confrontational in nature. Some cultures may also have difficulty with the emphasis on dreams, fantasies, and symbols, which may be foreign to many people and therefore may be incompatible with their orientation to the world.

40. **Answer: D** - A worldview, from the multicultural counseling viewpoint, is a set of beliefs or assumptions that describe reality for that person, or a perspective, both conscious and unconscious of the world. It is imperative that clinicians understand their worldview and how it may differ from a client's worldview and have the skills to minimize or adapt for those differences to keep them from interfering in the therapeutic process.

41. **Answer: A** - Environment plays an important role in human life by regulating growth and development. Specifically, environment can influence height, weight, and body structure. It can also influence intelligence, aptitude, and instincts.

42. **Answer: C** - All physical surroundings constitute a physical environment. The surroundings must be manipulated so as to provide basic necessities. Weather and climate are physical environments that have a major bearing on a child.

43. **Answer: D** -Three main types of environment are physical, social, and psychological. Social environment is made up of social laws and customs by which behavior is dictated. Psychological environment is an individual's interaction with an object.

44. **Answer: B** - Hormones are chemical substances secreted by an endocrine gland or group of endocrine cells that act to control or regulate specific physiological processes. Hormones have the power to speed up or slow down the activity level of the body or certain organs. Hormones regulate growth, metabolism, and reproduction.

45. **Answer: B** - Learning is the most relevant and basic topic in the science of psychology. Learning includes comprehension and aptitude, good and bad habits, associations, and attitudes people develop on a daily basis. Learning is an ongoing process.

46. **Answer: D** - Reinforcement is a major factor in growth and development. "We learn by doing" is a well-known psychological proverb. Activities should be repeated until the desired results are attained.

47. **Answer: B** - Charles Darwin believed that by observing child development, we may gain knowledge as to how the human species came about. He established that all species of life have come down through the years from common ancestors. Darwin published his theory of evolution in 1859.

48. **Answer: A** - Vygotsky insisted that children's minds are shaped by certain social and historical context in which they live as well as the children's interaction with adults. He believed that children are curious and involved in their own learning and development. Vygotsky placed more emphasis on social presence to child development as opposed to self-initiated discovery.

49. **Answer: C** - Human development is a lifelong process of physical, cognitive, and emotional growth and change. In the early stages of life enormous changes take place. Throughout life each individual incorporates learned attitudes and values to steer decisions, relationships, and comprehension.

50. **Answer: C** - A key component of emotional development in a toddler is developing trust for caregivers who provide for his or her needs. They will look to their caregivers to provide needs such as nourishment, comfort, and getting their diaper changed. The other answers are all part of cognitive development.

Helping Relationships

1. **Answer: D** - After many years sharing Freud's perspectives on human development and psychotherapy, Alfred Adler later became dissatisfied with the psychoanalysis focus and rigidity and developed what became known as *Individual Psychology*. This theory is based on social context, family dynamics, and child rearing. The goal of Adler's Individual Psychology is to comprehend the unique individual.

2. **Answer: D** - Avoiding the tar baby is an intervention designed to help people avoid those traps and places where they frequently get stuck. Spitting in the client's soup describes the identification of underlying motivations behind the client's self-defeating behaviors and then spoiling his or her imagined payoff by making it unappealing.

3. **Answer: C** - Lifestyle Assessment is one aspect of the phase of treatment known as Exploration and Analysis. Promoting Insight, Establishing a Therapeutic Relationship, and Change and Reorientation are additional phases of treatment in Adler's work. The other aspects of Exploration and Analysis are family constellations and birth order, dreams, earliest recollections, priorities, and ways of balancing.

4. **Answer: A** - Karen Horney's refusal to strictly adhere to Freudian theory resulted in her expulsion from the New York Psychoanalytic Institute, allowing her the freedom to organize a new group entitled the Association for the Advancement of Psychoanalysis.

5. **Answer: B** - Satir is often described as the master of communication. She believed that caring and affection were key elements in helping people face their fears and move into a more open approach to others in the family. She is one of the key figures in the development of family therapy. She died in 1988 after a long and fruitful career.

6. **Answer: C** - Rationalization is one of the basic psychoanalytic defense mechanisms found in the category of neurotic defenses. These mechanisms are common in most people, according to psychoanalytic theory, and they can be a key to underlying problem areas in the ego.

7. **Answer: B** - A defense mechanism is primarily used to protect people from anxiety, particularly anxiety arising from unacceptable wishes and impulses. Everyone has defenses and some are healthy and mature, such as sublimation, which can change an unhealthy, self-destructive desire into the drive to create a work of art. Others are unhealthy and can distort reality, interfering in efforts to build relationships.

8. **Answer: D** - The main focus of Bowen's family theory is to bring about change in the individual and the couple. To facilitate such change in both the individual and the couple, the theory concentrates on the balance of two forces: individuality and togetherness. A distant and estranged family is caused by too much individuality, whereas fusion is created by too much togetherness and prevents individuality. Bowen's family theory seeks to create a balance of the two for a healthy family.

9. **Answer: C** - Carl Whitaker's approach to family therapy was called experiential. Whitaker believed in the 'here and now' and often used a confrontational approach in therapy. He believed that the relationship between the therapist and the family was more important than a particular psychological theory.

10. **Answer: C** - One of the primary goals in Whitaker's Experiential Family Therapy is to reduce defensiveness within the family members and unlock deeper levels of experiencing in order to improve communication and ultimately reduce conflict.

11. **Answer: D** - Each of the answer choices listed is a criticism of this theory. Modern clinicians are aware of weaknesses in the ideas of object relations theories. On the other hand, these theories have made many important contributions to counseling and psychotherapy. Object relations theories can be seen in the application of play therapy, art therapy, and group therapy.

12. **Answer: C** - Research on Brief Psychodynamic Therapy has shown it to be helpful in treating Depression. Brief psychodynamic therapy is much shorter than traditional analysis and centers on a focal concern that seems to be linked to the person's symptoms. Goals in this type of therapy are clear and circumscribed.

13. **Answer: D** - In-depth dream interpretation might be a part of psychoanalytic therapy, but is not a goal for brief psychodynamic therapy. In BPT, the therapist plays an active role in helping people lead more rewarding lives, focusing on promoting insight into current problems, eliciting feelings, and promoting new learning in order to accomplish the ultimate goal of reducing symptoms of the focal concern.

14. **Answer: A** - Humanism views people as capable and autonomous, with the ability to resolve their difficulties, realize their potential, and change their lives in positive ways.

15. **Answer: B** - Carl Rogers is the father of person-centered counseling. According to him understanding, appreciating, and relating to others in positive ways were the ultimate goals. The theory of person-centered counseling reflects this. Erikson created the eight stages of development, Karl Marx was a socialist, and Carl Jung created Jungian analytical psychology.

16. **Answer: A** - Existential therapy is focused on helping people find value, meaning, and purpose in their lives. A part of this is to facilitate change where needed, but it is not the fundamental goal. Understanding ego defense mechanisms is a part of psychoanalytic therapy.

17. **Answer: B** - If I were a Gestalt therapist, I would use the type of therapeutic treatment known as role play. Spitting in the client's soup is an Adlerian therapeutic intervention; reflection is used in Psychodynamic therapy; and visualization is used in Focus-Oriented psychotherapy.

18. **Answer: D** - Typical goals in therapy might include all of the options listed. The main focus of Gestalt therapy is to promote the natural growth of the person and enable them to live aware and actualized lives and to help clients feel more fulfilled and whole.

19. **Answer: C** - In Narrative therapy, people are seen as interpretive beings who can make meaning of their world through the language of their own stories. Narrative theorists believe that through exploration, deconstruction, and revision of personal stories, people can shift their perceptions, leading to greater empowerment and the ability to successfully manage their lives.

20. **Answer: C** - Narrative therapy seems particularly well suited for treatment of people who have been victimized, such as women, the elderly, and individuals from ethnic and cultural groups. It can also be beneficial in dealing with eating disorders, addressing marital conflict, and for people dealing with grief. It is not beneficial when people are in crisis or those seeking a quick solution for a specific problem.

21. **Answer: A** - Cognitive therapy differs from the others because it focuses on the way people think, not the way people feel. Cognitive therapists believe that the basic material of treatment is people transient automatic thoughts and their deeply ingrained assumptions.

22. **Answer: D** - Aaron Beck is the man behind the development of cognitive therapy. He was trained as a psychoanalyst, but soon gravitated toward an approach that emphasized cognitions (thoughts). Gestalt therapy and existential therapy are the work of many people and Carl Rogers is seen as the founder of person-centered therapy.

23. **Answer: C**- An understanding of past relationships is not an element in a case formulation. An understanding of background relevant to development of the core belief, however, is an element of case formulation, as are the others listed above.

24. **Answer: D** - All of the choices listed in this question are categories of distorted thinking. All-or-nothing thinking is viewing a situation in terms of extremes, rather than on a continuum. Overgeneralization draws sweeping conclusions that are not justified by the evidence and emotional reasoning believes that something is true just because it feels that way.

25. **Answer: A** - Albert Ellis is the originator of REBT, Rational Emotive Behavior Therapy. He began practicing marriage and family therapy in the 1940s and was a believer in psychoanalysis as a way to help people achieve profound change. He eventually became dissatisfied with the inefficiency of this approach and began to search for a way to treat people that focused on their thoughts.

26. **Answer: A** - By identifying, evaluating, and if needed, changing thought patterns, cognitive therapists empower people to make positive changes. The process gives such people the skills needed to overcome distorted thoughts that contribute to problems. It is a time-limited, structured approach that offers specific plans for change.

27. **Answer: B** - Research indicates that cognitive therapy is particularly effective in treating depression and anxiety. It is also effective with a broad range of other mental disorders where distorted thoughts may be contributing to the concern.

28. **Answer: C** - Didactic dispute is not one of the four strategies of disputation in REBT. Logical disputes identify magical thinking, empirical disputes focus on the accumulation of evidence, and rational alternative beliefs offer a viable alternative belief to a possible explanation. The last of the four strategies of disputation are the functional disputing strategies that focus on the practical consequences of people's beliefs.

29. **Answer: A** - EMDR, or Eye Movement Desensitization and Reprocessing, is a form of treatment using directed eye movements and other guided tracking procedures to accelerate people's processing of negative information and enable them to deal with that information in new ways that promote their emotional health.

30. **Answer: A** - The meta-analysis showed EMDR to be more efficient in treating PTSD than other treatments, including drug treatment. However, other research has shown it to be effective for other disorders as well, including depression, anxiety, substance use, sexual dysfunction, and somatoform disorders. It works equally well in children and adults.

31. **Answer: B** - One specific treatment goal is to reduce the perfectionism and rigidity of the superego. The overall goal of psychoanalysis is for the ego to function with the best possible psychological equilibrium. Another goal might be developing a capacity for healthy and rewarding intimate relationships, along with the ability to express oneself in rewarding ways.

32. **Answer: B** - Jungian analysis is deep and intensive, encouraging the emergence and understanding of material from both the personal and the collective unconscious. It ultimately leads to the resolution of inner conflicts, greater balance, and integration in the person.

33. **Answer: A** - Jungian treatment typically involves catharsis, elucidation, education, and transformation. Catharsis involves the discharge of strong emotions. Elucidation clarifies the meaning of symptoms and much analysis is done at this stage. Education is intended to remedy any gaps in development or maturation that have resulted from maladjustment. Transformation occurs when the person has greater access to the collective unconscious. It allows for an ego-self dialogue, creating further emergence of the self and greater balance.

34. **Answer: C** - TA has its roots in psychoanalytic theory, but reaches toward the humanistic approaches. It deemphasizes the unconscious and instead, focuses on responsibility, emotional health, and social relationships throughout life. It does, however, maintain that development is formed primarily in the early years and by parental messages.

35. **Answer: D** - Eric Berne developed Transactional Analysis. This psychologist was interested in both traditional psychoanalysis and research on the electrical stimulation of the brain, which led him to believe that people could re-experience previous thoughts and emotions in a vivid way.

36. **Answer: D** - All of the choices listed in this questions were identified by Holden as impediments to people's personal and transpersonal development that keep the higher self-underdeveloped or repressed. The fourth block to development is Impotence (internal and external constraints on access to options). Holden refers to these blocks as the "Four I's" and she recommends assessing people's physical, interpersonal, intrapersonal, and transpersonal realms.

37. **Answer: C** - B.F. Skinner was an experimental psychologist and perhaps the best-known behavioral theorist. His ideas are known as *operant reinforcement theory*,which postulates that the frequency of a behavior being emitted is largely determined by the events that follow that behavior.

38. **Answer: D** - Ivan Pavlov is well known for his study of the process of using conditioning with dogs. Pavlov, a Russian physiologist, identified and wrote about a type of learning that has become known as *classical conditioning*. He demonstrated that, by simultaneously presenting an unconditioned stimulus (meat paste) and a conditioned stimulus (the sound of a tuning fork); researchers could eventually elicit the dogs' response of salivation by using the conditioned stimulus (tuning fork) without the presence of the conditioned stimulus (meat paste). In other words, eventually the dogs' salivated just on hearing the tuning fork.

39. **Answer: B** - Classical and operant conditioning are both an integral part of social learning in behavior therapy. Bandura found that learning and subsequent behavior change could occur vicariously through observation of other people's behaviors. This process is called *modeling.*

40. **Answer: D** - Cognitive therapy alone is not one of the models of behavior therapy. However, there is a combined theory called cognitive behavior therapy, which is one of the models and looks at how cognitions shape behaviors and emotions. Applied behavior analysis looks at the impact of environmental events on behavior. Social learning theory seeks to understand the interaction of cognitive, behavioral, and environmental factors in shaping behavior, and Neo-behaviorism focuses on the process of conditioning or learning responses.

41. **Answer: A** - Two steps in behavioral therapy treatment involve conceptualizing the problem and developing strategies to facilitate change. Using this therapy, a patient will first conceptualize the problem by reviewing the nature of the problem and its history and exploring the context of the unwanted behavior. Then, the patient will develop strategies to facilitate change by learning skills that can contribute to the change and by anticipating precipitating conditions that trigger undesirable behaviors.

42. **Answer: C** - One of the main goals of behavior therapy is to extinguish maladaptive behaviors and help people learn new adaptive ones. Some areas where behavior therapy can be effective include abstinence from drugs and alcohol, reduction in nail biting, improvement in social skills, and weight loss.

43. **Answer: B** - Reality therapy was initially developed by William Glasser in the 1960s and is solidly grounded in cognitive and behavioral theory and interventions. Reality therapy focuses on the present and seeks to help people make changes in their thoughts and actions in order for them to lead more rewarding lives.

44. **Answer: C** - Glasser believed that people have two basic needs; relatedness (to love and be loved) and respect (to feel worthwhile to oneself and others). The founder of Reality therapy, Glasser utilized both cognitive and behavior theories in Reality therapy.

45. **Answer: D** - WDEP is the acronym for Wants, Directions and Doing, Evaluation, and Planning. These are not sequential, but can be applied in whatever way seems most likely to be helpful. NLPT is an acronym for neurolinguistic programming, AARP is short for the American Association for Retired Persons and EMDR is an acronym for eye movement desensitization and reprocessing.

46. **Answer: D** - Answer choices A and C both describe Multimodal Therapy. Lazarus encouraged clinicians to draw on an array of theories and strategies to match treatment to client and problem. Its emphasis on outcomes draws heavily on cognitive therapy, as well as social learning theory.

47. **Answer: D** - All of the answer choices might cause a clinician to decide to use an Eclectic approach to counseling. Despite attempting to identify one theory as better than all the rest, it has not been found. However, much research has shown that certain types of therapy do work better than others for certain types of problems (i.e., depression responds very well to Cognitive therapy, while nail biting is resolved through Behavior therapy).

48. **Answer: B** - Existential therapy is not problem focused and involves the establishment of a deep relationship between client and clinician. As a result, it is almost never time limited or rushed. Typically, no clear stages or transitions can be identified in the treatment. Within this treatment, people use the information they have shared about themselves to find meaning in their lives.

49. **Answer: A** - For existential therapists, self-actualization is an important concept, as it is for person-centered therapists. Abraham Maslow describes the nature of self-actualization as that of fulfilling potential, reaching for the highest within, and growing from within.

50. **Answer: D** - Cognitions can be categorized according to four levels; automatic thoughts, intermediate beliefs, core beliefs, and schemas. In cognitive therapy, treatment typically begins with automatic thoughts and then proceeds to identification, evaluation, and modification of intermediate and core beliefs and finally, of schemas.

Research and Program Evaluation

1. **Answer: C** - The three basic elements to look for when assessing a psychology test are reliability, validity, and standardization. Reliability is a measure of test consistency, validity is a measure of test usefulness, and standardization provides a mean (average) and a standard deviation (spread) relative to a certain group.

2. **Answer: C** - An item characteristic curve plots the probability of answering an item correctly against estimates of ability

3. **Answer: A** - In teach-made tests, an item analysis is important because it reveals correctable features in the test teaching. Such analysis provides the opportunity to improve teaching methods going forward.

4. **Answer: B** - Self-report personality tests such as the androgyny scale or the locus of control scale tests one specific personality trait. These tests are generally used for research.

5. **Answer: D** - A Phrenology expert would test your personality by studying the bumps on your head. It was widely used in the 1800's but is still used today - primarily by pseudo-psychologists. In the 1800's, a respected person would carefully measure and examine your skull. Then you would be given a psychological profile of your unique qualities and characteristics. Phrenologists used a phrenology chart to determine which personality traits were associated with bumps on different areas of the skull.

6. **Answer: C** - Basic research uses the goals of psychology to study behavior simply for knowledge. In other words, basic research studies theoretical questions without trying to solve a specific problem.

7. **Answer: D** - Applied research is not done for study purposes. Applied research is research that utilizes the principles and discoveries of psychology for practical purposes or to solve real-world problems.

8. **Answer: B** - In the realm of psychological research, hypotheses and variables belong to research methodology. A hypothesis gives a possible explanation of an experimental problem before an experiment is conducted. Variables are representations of a measurable trait in an experiment. Some variables can be controlled and some cannot be controlled.

9. **Answer: C** - A Theory combines interrelated sets of concepts in an attempt to explain the body of data that was gathered and to generate testable hypotheses.

10. **Answer: D** - An experiment is a carefully controlled scientific procedure conducted to determine if certain variables manipulated by the experimenter have an effect on other variables.

11. **Answer: A** - An Independent variable is controlled by the experimenter and is applied to the participant to determine its effect.

12. **Answer: D** - A Placebo is a substance that would normally produce no physiological effect that is used as a control technique, usually in drug research.

13. **Answer: C** - The Placebo Effect is a change in the participants' behavior brought about because they believe they have received a drug that elicits that change when in reality they have received a placebo, an inert substance.

14. **Answer: D** - Experimenter bias is the tendency of experimenters to influence the results of a research study in the expected direction.

15. **Answer: A** - A sample is a selected group of participants that is representative of a larger population from which the group was selected.

16. **Answer: B** - A hypothesis is a tentative explanation of the behavior to be researched.

17. **Answer: B -** In an experiment, researchers isolate one single factor and examine the effect of it alone on a behavior.

18. **Answer: C** - Surveys are a non-experimental research technique. This method offers a researcher a way to study a wide variety of behaviors and attitudes without conducting an experiment.

19. **Answer: D** - When researchers systematically record the behavior of participants in their natural state or habitat it is referred to as naturalistic observation. This natural state or habitat may be a jungle full of chimpanzees, a classroom of high school students, or a mother in her kitchen.

20. **Answer: C** - A case study is an in-depth study of a single subject. In a case study, many aspects of a person's life are examined in depth in an attempt to describe the person's behavior and to evaluate techniques that may be used.

21. **Answer: B** - Correlational research does not have internal validity, so no causal relationships can be determined. Causal relationships can be inferred in some instances. Correlational research can measure the strength of dependence between two variables that is not otherwise accounted for (causally, or by their response to other variables).

22. **Answer: B** - Multiple baseline design is used when reversal is not possible. This design addresses the ethical concerns of withholding a potentially-helpful treatment from a subject or withdrawing treatment that has proven to be helpful while the study is still underway.

23. **Answer: A** - Case studies are not used to measure attitude, preferences, and satisfaction, because those data are quantitative rather than qualitative. Surveys (which are quantitative research) are used to measure attitude, preferences, and satisfaction.

24. **Answer: A** - Meta-analysis quantifies findings of multiple studies by applying empirical methods to available literature. Effect size is a result of meta-analysis. Meta-analysis is not part of a study itself, but uses the results of many studies.

25. **Answer: C** - A study comparing alcohol consumption rates between adolescent males and females is observational research. Observational, or non-experimental, research does not involve manipulation or intervention. This type of research studies independent variables (like gender) that cannot be manipulated combined with dependent variables that are not manipulated (alcohol consumption). Other types of research include more intervention.

26. **Answer: D** - Within subjects design sometimes requires the process of counterbalancing. This type of design refers to comparing groups that are related or correlated in some manner, such as from repeat measurements. Repeated measure design (one type of within subjects design) requires counterbalancing because of possible carryover effects between each measurement.

27. **Answer: B** - Mixed design involves groups that are both correlated and independent. With this design, patients are assigned to different treatment groups (independent) and each group is measured more than once (correlated).

28. **Answer: A** - Autocorrelation, which refers to the effect of measuring one individual repeatedly, is a significant problem in single-subject design. Autocorrelation is likely to produce scores that do not accurately reflect the research variables.

29. **Answer: A** - Time investment and financial investment are problems associated with multiple baseline design. AB design carries the threat of history-it is hard to determine whether intervention or another event caused change. Ethical concerns and the failure of a dependent variable to return to baseline are both problems associated with ABAB design.

30. **Answer: A** - Instrumentation refers to changes in researchers or calibration of equipment used in a study, and it is a threat to internal validity. It is a factor other than the independent variable that might affect the dependent variable of a study.

31. **Answer: A** - The Hawthorne effect is a threat to external validity. Threats to external validity are factors that interfere with the ability of research to determine if results can be generalized to the population. The Hawthorne effect is a specific example of the threat of reactivity (which is a type of contextual characteristic threat). Reactivity involves subjects behaving in certain ways because they know they are being observed.

32.

Answer: C - Causal research studies the possibility of one variable being the reason another variable happens or changes. Research on cause and effect is the most well-known scientific experiment. An example of this type of research would be altering the treatment of one variable and studying the effects the alteration causes.

33.

Answer: D - Descriptive research attempts to portray what presently exists in a group or population. for example, an opinion survey to determine whether or not a particular service is needed in a community is a type of descriptive research. Descriptive research does not try to measure the effect of a variable, only to describe it.

34.

Answer: A - Relational research is a study that examines the correlation between two or more variables. The variables which are examined are usually already present in the group. for example, a study that tracks the number of males and females that would attend either a baseball or football game would be studying the relationship between gender and sports preference.

35. **Answer: A** - Applied research is a form of research which focuses on solving practical problems. It uses parts of accumulated theories, knowledge, methods, and techniques for a specific reason. Applied research is interested in finding answers to problems that impact daily life.

36. **Answer: C** - The Hawthorne effect is a term that refers to the tendency of some people to work harder and perform better when participating in an experiment. Individuals may alter their actions because of the attention they receive from researchers instead of any manipulation of independent variables. The term gets its name from a factory called the Hawthorne Works where a series of experiments on factory workers was done between 1924 and 1932.

37. **Answer: B** - The Scientific method is a set of principles and procedures used by researchers to develop questions, collect data, and come to conclusions. The goal of a researcher is to describe behaviors and explain why they happen. They also try to do research which can be utilized to predict and possibly modify human behavior

38. **Answer: D** - Cross-sectional research is observational and known as descriptive research as opposed to causal or relational. This type of study utilizes various groups of people who differ in the variable of interest, but share other characteristics. Cross-sectional research may be used to describe characteristics that exist in a population, but not for determining cause-and-effect relationships between variables.

39. **Answer: D** - Some negative factors regarding longitudinal research are longitudinal research needs large quantities of time and can become a financial drain. Due in part to this, studies sometimes have just a small group of participants, making it harder to relate the results to a larger group. An additional issue is that participants often drop out of the research due to the length of the study, leaving the sample group even smaller.

40. **Answer: D** - Panel studies, cohort studies, and retrospective studies are all types of longitudinal research. Panel studies involve testing a wide variety of individuals, whereas cohort studies involve selecting participants based on a mutual event such as birth or location. Retrospective studies entail searching the past by studying historical data such as medical records.

41. **Answer: A** - An advantage of naturalistic observation is that it may be the only option if a lab is not available. Naturalistic observation can be done in any setting and gives the observer the benefit of viewing the subject in natural surroundings. It can also offer direction into ongoing research.

42. **Answer: B** - The survey method is one of the most common tools used in psychological research. Because this method is easy and affordable, researchers can gather large quantities of information quickly. The survey method is more flexible than its counterparts.

43. **Answer: D** - Operant conditioning is also known as instrumental conditioning. It is a mode of learning which happens through rewards and punishment for behavior. A link is made between an act and a consequence of that act.

44. **Answer: D** - Harvard psychologist Howard Gardener is responsible for the multiple intelligences theory. The theory suggests traditional views of intelligence are too confining. Gardener suggested there are eight and possibly nine intelligences.

45. **Answer: A** - A demand characteristic is a subtle hint that lets clients know what the researcher expects to discover or how he or she expects the client to react. Researchers rely on a broad range of procedures to help lessen demand characteristics, including deception. This is comprised of making the client think the researcher is studying one thing while, in fact, the researcher is observing something entirely different.

46. **Answer: C** - The converger style is one of David Kolb's four learning styles. People with this learning style have superior aptitudes in the fields of abstract conceptualization and active experimentation and are greatly adept in implementing ideas. They tend to excel in circumstances where there is one best answer or solution to an issue.

47. **Answer: A** - The primary focus of the Middendorf Breath Experience is to discover the body's own natural responses and sensation to the breath as it comes and goes. An individual practicing this technique is inspired to focus in the now and be attuned to other feelings such as imagination, feeling or thinking. By concentrating only on sensory perception, the client is able to gain knowledge into how reactions are developed and processed.

48. **Answer: C** - In classical conditioning, extinction happens when a stimulus is no longer paired with an unconditioned stimulus. For example, if the smell of food (the unconditioned stimulus) had been paired with the sound of a whistle (the conditioned stimulus), it would sooner or later come to induce the conditioned response of hunger. However, if the conditioned stimulus (the whistle) was no longer teamed with the unconditioned stimulus (the smell of food), eventually the conditioned response (hunger) would vanish.

49. **Answer: D** - None of the answers provided fit the description for this question. A double-blind study is one which neither the researcher nor the participant knows who is receiving a particular treatment. This type of study is used to avoid bias in research results. Double-blind studies are especially helpful for preventing bias due to demand characteristics or the placebo effect.

95967273R00089

Made in the USA
Columbia, SC
18 May 2018